brilliant

How to solve problems and make brilliant decisions

PEARSON

At Pearson, we take learning personally. Our courses and resources are available as books, online and via multi-lingual packages, helping people learn whatever, wherever and however they choose.

We work with leading authors to develop the strongest learning experiences, bringing cutting-edge thinking and best learning practice to a global market. We craft our print and digital resources to do more to help learners not only understand their content, but to see it in action and apply what they learn, whether studying or at work.

Pearson is the world's leading learning company. Our portfolio includes Penguin, Dorling Kindersley, the Financial Times and our educational business, Pearson International. We are also a leading provider of electronic learning programmes and of test development, processing and scoring services to educational institutions, corporations and professional bodies around the world.

Every day our work helps learning flourish, and wherever learning flourishes, so do people.

To learn more please visit us at: www.pearson.com/uk

How to solve problems and make brilliant decisions

Creative thinking skills that really work

Richard Hall

PEARSON

Harlow, England • London • New York • Boston • San Francisco • Toronto • Sydney
Auckland • Singapore • Hong Kong • Tokyo • Seoul • Taipei • New Delhi
Cape Town • São Paulo • Mexico City • Madrid • Amsterdam • Munich • Paris • Milan

PEARSON EDUCATION LIMITED

Edinburgh Gate
Harlow CM20 2JE
United Kingdom
Tel: +44 (0)1279 623623
Web: www.pearson.com/uk

First edition published 2015 (print and electronic)

© Pearson Education Limited 2015 (print and electronic)

The right of Richard Hall to be identified as author of this work has been asserted by him in accordance with the Copyright, Designs and Patents Act 1988.

Pearson Education is not responsible for the content of third-party internet sites.

ISBN: 978–1–292–06402–4 (print)
       978–1–292–06404–8 (PDF)
       978–1–292–06405–5 (ePub)
       978–1–292–06403–1 (eText)

British Library Cataloguing-in-Publication Data
A catalogue record for the print edition is available from the British Library

Library of Congress Cataloging-in-Publication Data
Hall, Richard, 1944-
  How to solve problems and make brilliant decisions : creative thinking skills that really work / Richard Hall.
    pages cm. -- (Brilliant)
  Includes index.
  ISBN 978-1-292-06402-4 (softcover)
  1. Decision making. 2. Problem solving. I. Title.
  HD30.23.H345 2015
  658.4'03--dc23
                      2014034208

10 9 8 7 6 5 4 3 2 1
18 17 16 15 14

Cover design by David Carroll & Co
Print edition typeset in 10/14pt by 3
Print edition printed and bound in Malaysia

NOTE THAT ANY PAGE CROSS REFERENCES REFER TO THE PRINT EDITION

Contents

About the author

Richard Hall read English at Balliol College, Oxford before venturing enthusiastically into marketing and then advertising. Since 2000 he has split his time between consulting, coaching and writing numerous books for Pearson, all on business. He lives in Brighton surrounded by family, great nieces and grandchildren.

He claims to be thinking a lot – hence this book – but it's likely he's just having a rather good time.

Preface

All around me as I was writing this book I found a rash of new books and talks on radio, TV and on stage about neuroscience and aspects of thinking. I read and heard about mindfulness, intuition, insight, systems one, two and even system three, and (extraordinarily) a child's book. This was about a nit that enters a child's brain and finding lots of unused brain space there has conversations with the child inside his head to change his focus and ability.

So thinking is the very zeitgeist thing and I was on that roller coaster.

What I've discovered is my life has been changed by thinking about thinking.

Most of all, although I'd thought I'd been thinking effectively, I was, in fact, operating well under par most of the time, underpowered by failing to have sufficient balance between my rational mind and my intuitive mind. I was simply unaware that I had this heavyweight genius in my skull that I was treating rather like an uncooperative tradesman.

Daniel Kahneman is the Nobel prize-winning name that constantly comes up in this field. He has been a guide and mentor through his writing and talking. But he's not alone. Almost whoever I've read, listened or spoken to has something to add, to ask or to argue with.

What lies in our heads and which is working in there 24/7/365 (there's no day of rest for our brains) is more complex, more interesting and more creative than any of us could imagine.

If this book helps further the cause of thinking about thinking and specifically helps people be better at what they do at work by thinking faster and more clearly, well that is the goal.

It's my belief that in a knowledge economy where the tools of technology allow us to think more and process less, it is our job to improve our cognitive skills. For my part, my mission and desire is to shove people enthusiastically along the adventurous path of clearer, more exciting, effective and creative thinking.

My thanks to my patient wife whose morning slumbers would be broken by my haranguing her about the latest insight I'd had: 'Do you have to talk about thinking when I've just woken up and can't begin to think?' And my thanks especially for the guidance, intelligence and encouragement of my commissioning editor Steve Temblett. A thinker and a cricket lover. It's helped the process for me.

And finally to all the people to whom I talked and who fed me so many thoughts.

So here's the book. What do you think?

Richard Hall, November 2014
www.colourfulthinkers.com

hallogram.richard@gmail.com
http://marketing-creativity-leadership.blogspot.co.uk/

Introduction: what do you think?

We live in a world where employers want more smart workers and less sweaty work. They want their people to develop their thinking skills so they get better solutions – better, clearer decisions. They are looking for executives who think about how to get the best out of each other. People who think better in their workplace, when they write, when they talk, in interviews, wherever; quite simply these people will do better if they think better. By out-thinking competition, anticipating change and inventing new creative solutions we can train our brain to think the way to greater success.

So what do you think?

Possibly the four most loaded words in our vocabulary are those when you ask 'what do you think?' This can mean 'what's your opinion?' or 'what have you decided?' or, when used indignantly, as in 'what do *you* think?' meaning 'isn't that obvious to any idiot?' We also recognise the real power of thought when we suggest to people 'think about it' or, in rebuke, 'what *were* you thinking about?'

An absence of thinking is regarded as bad and the need for active thinking has become increasingly important in a complex world where even the cleverest people seem barely able to cope.

Active thinking will mark you out and make a difference and it can be learned. So what do you think?

It really hurts, thinking does

Thinking's hard to do because it's an unaccustomed activity for many people. Active thinking is driven by our emotions, although we seem to hope when we actually do think that we are being deeply forensic and rational. Sorry, no. All the work done by psychologists shows it's our intuition – a slippery, now-you-see-it-now-you-don't, emotional facet – that really controls our thinking. Our intuition works fast and, I'm afraid, slightly carelessly helped by its younger, junior and rather lazy cousin, our rational mind.

This harsh reality needs to be borne in mind throughout this book. Our brains are not infallible computers. They are slightly careless, slightly lazy, magical tools that can dream up poetry, art, jokes and do difficult sums but they are not perfect. Nor are they completely trustworthy having a propensity, for instance, to rewrite history. But the more you learn about them the more fantastic they seem.

But when we understand what's really going on inside our head, we also realise that controlling our first impressions and training our gut or our instincts is the starting point to becoming a better thinker. Research shows our unconscious is at work in decision-making prior to our conscious mind engaging, so whilst we might like to think we're coolly rational, trust me we're not.

The world today is noisy with the crash of breaking news. We live in 'do-do' times and deep thinking is as out of fashion as is deep reading[1] (by the way, we read less than the French and Americans) and carefully, structured, thoughtful writing of which we see less and less. We tweet and we skim. We do not ponder because pondering is, well it's sort of, ponderous and old fashioned.

So, yes, thinking hard hurts. What I'm going to try to do is help you get good enough to think through the pain. You are like an athlete who through lack of mental exercise needs a workout (and more). Through a process of training, discipline and visualisation, your brain can be trained to work more brilliantly. More importantly it can be trained to (as it were) turn up on time and do what you need it to much more reliably.

The two big topics: emotion and e-motion

So we have to accept, for better or worse, that an awful lot of thinking is emotional rather than rational. But now another emotional player has turned up. This other 'emotion' is critical to thinking today. 'E-motion' is changing our lives and those around us. 'E-motion' is what the power of the web creates, a web controlled extensively by the young. (And certainly without the support of the Facebook generation it's going to be remarkably hard to get things done in the future.)

By the way, if at this moment you are wondering if you can outsource your thinking, forget it. Thinking is a strictly DIY activity. It's what you and your wonderful mind dream up that's going to matter. You may be able to buy in consultancy for IT and accountancy but not the power to outthink your competitors. (Actually I did hear someone rather chillingly say his company had got Ernst and Young in 'to help us with our thinking'. But that, of course, was before we thought of writing this book.)

E-motion is what Rory Sutherland[2] was talking about when recently, amplifying Daniel Kahneman's System 1, System 2 thesis from his book *Thinking Fast, Thinking Slow* (don't worry I'll explain this in more detail later on but for the moment System 1 = emotional thinking, System 2 = rational thinking), Rory added an extra one – System 3. It's the computing power mankind has at its fingertips and the momentum its brain power allied to the power of the computer can achieve together. So here it is simply:

Emotion drives our thinking. E-motion gives us the power to execute those thoughts reliably, consistently and fast.

If you like mindfulness you've got to try thoughtfulness

Given the stress so many people seem to be feeling it's no surprise that 'mindfulness', by which I mean focusing on the present and not regretting the past nor being in terror of an uncertain future, has gained so much traction. And isn't it comforting that when talking about stress, even in France, that relaxed and linguistically proud country, people talk about 'le burnout'?

'Mindfulness' courses, I've heard, are so fashionable now, especially amongst male executives, that the concept is described as being 'the new black'. 'Mindfulness' has become a multi-million pound business inspired, amongst others, by Gwyneth Paltrow who spoke about it at Davos. And mindfulness works. It calms people down and really helps them focus on what they have to do and get done now.

Well I have a *new improved* concept, and remember that you heard it here first. I think it's an improvement but it's actually complementary. It's '**thoughtfulness**'.

- If mindfulness is the new black then thoughtfulness is the new technicolour.
- Use those 100+ billion neurons in our brain to greater effect and slow down that perverse urge to break the thinking speed limit.
- Think about new, different, unthought of things; working things out; balancing the pros and cons; sitting or walking and waiting as you search for the right word, the right metaphor or the right piece of evidence.

Meet the thought police

No, the 'thought police' are not my version of the 'Stasi' or creatures from an Orwellian world. They are just, instead, a self-created check on speed thinking. Speed thinking? Yes, that's the alpha urge to put your mental foot down and, making a series of intuitive leaps, rather like a boy-racer high on dopamine, propel yourself from 'A to Z' very fast and rather dangerously. It's time to be pulled over and asked in a laid back, ironic way by these thought police: 'Late for *Mastermind* this evening are we Sir?'

Most of us make decisions much faster than we need to.

Few of us stop and just think a bit longer and a bit harder.

Fewer of us still let ideas sit in the Aga of our minds, nicely stewing away.

Why this omission? Because, quite simply, we've forgotten *how* to think. We are prisoners in a got-to-get-it-done world where (or so we think) the sum of all human knowledge is on our mobile phone. And when we delegate our thinking to an iPhone it's time to, well, think again: 'On your way Sir and please think about what you're doing next time.'

The urge for and problem with oversimplification

Our very human mind finds it appealing to create stories or conspiracy theories where none actually exist. It does not appreciate the idea of 'random' but prefers to discover patterns and use simplifying devices like runes and rhymes:

'Just read this book and have no fear it'll help you think and change your career.'

It's strange but expressed like that it conveys a possibility of truth that the blunt 'read this and get on' will not. The latter sells, the former wraps up the thought in a kind of irrefutable, pseudo-biblical parcel.

Myers Briggs,[3] a system strongly advocated by many, does just that too. For those who don't know about it, it's the personality checking system beloved of HR people. If you haven't been Myers Brigged then you probably haven't got a personality in the accepted sense of the word. Ironically it identifies around the same number of types of personality as the number of behaviours performed by the Mexican Green Lizard that have been identified by Californian PhD students. That's 27.

Well I may be perverse but I think there are more than 27 personality types. I think it's the diversity of people and their attitudes and behaviour that makes humanity so fascinating. So, yes, I am very cautious about oversimplification.

The more one studies the brain and the process of thinking the more the tendency to dumb down and pigeonhole seems inappropriate because it is so complex, so magical and so surprising that a bit of messiness in describing it seems not only right, but seems to capture the brain's ability to juggle and dance in a bizarre way.

In fact Martin Sorrell who runs the advertising giant WPP nailed it when he said:

'The 21st Century is not for tidy minds.'

There are two so-called laws of psychology worth bearing in mind here. 'Occam's Razor' which espouses simplification (in an acceptable way) in suggesting that it's the simplest cause of an event that is likeliest to be the true one. Experience would tend to confirm this is generally true, but with the proviso that the second law of 'Occam's Broom' doesn't also apply. This is the urge to sweep inconvenient evidence under the carpet that seems to disprove 'Occam's Razor'.[4]

This book has been a product of recursive thinking amongst other things. Recursive thinking is when you're thinking about thinking or, to make it even more complex, thinking about what you're thinking about thinking. This is something that dogs and even primates just can't do; they operate instead on a 'that's-a-bone-I'll-go-and-get-it' basis. But humans have unexplored thinking capacity and the next few pages are about trying to help unlock some of that potential.

There should however be great relief when I say the book is about how to think better in your workplace not how to think in a self-help way about creating a better life or improving your sex life; it neither seeks to preach nor embarks on intellectual debates (we'll leave that to Californian PhDs).

No. It seeks to find thinking solutions for people in business.

'Plus ça change' to all those who see revolution about to happen

The French seem to believe in the immutability of much of life, that the more things seem to change the more they remain the same. Certainly in some other places there's a widespread and misplaced belief that we are going through such a period of unheard of transformation that our current thinking equipment can't cope at all.

Interestingly there are some rules of life that are unchanging and rather like gravity pull trends back to their norms, pretty compellingly:

- Regression to the mean (meaning one day Apple and Google will get their come-uppance). A constant growth curve will, in other words, tend to self-correct.
- When under stress people revert to type. The actors on the business stage will appear in their true lights in a crisis.
- Business, carve up the mission statements however you will, is primarily there to make money; yes there's more to it than just that but when the crunch comes not that much more (ask Warren Buffett).

These gravitational pulls should help us when we are told that things today are very different and the old rules don't apply any more. As in football, baseball or rugby there are small and often important changes to the rules but the basic principles still apply. Do not be bamboozled by jargon or the latest trend. Experience shows that fewer things have changed than the media would like to think.

When confronted with explosive new news which seems to change all previous truth just think very hard. Think back to the last revelation. Think about the real odds of this news actually being true.

Why you'll enjoy thinking better

Edward de Bono (one of the original gurus of thinking and creativity) said:

 'Thinking is the ultimate human resource... the main difficulty is confusion, we try and do too much at once.'

Confusion is something I want to dispel in this book. As I've said I don't want to oversimplify things but I do want to help promote the idea of the sheer power that concentrated thought can bring to bear on problems we all encounter.

Learning how to think more clearly, more decisively and more creatively will improve your performance at and your enjoyment of work. The key is focus and structure. You cannot write a useful document or report that doesn't have a beginning, a middle and an end – and that doesn't seem to know where it's going. Equally the process of thinking needs an active plan to create structure, focus and purpose. I want you to become active thinkers not just passively thoughtful.

Inside our head neurons are firing away like children waiting for a trip to the seaside. They want to rush things, constantly crying 'are we there yet?' We can help ourselves by playing calm adult and setting out the problem in our own words carefully and fully so the thinking process doesn't start with the dessert and then move on to the first course followed by a fight and tears of recrimination.

Creative thinking is when we can let our minds off their leash a bit more. Here the task in the first instance is a burst of prolific idea generation progressing through to the most useful process of all – saying 'no' to the also-ran ideas and editing what's left. As Steve Jobs said, 'innovation is in saying "no" to a thousand things'. And don't underestimate the difficulty of saying 'no'. Research shows the more we think about and understand something like a business idea or a new product, the more we tend to believe in it.

That high that runners get with the release of endorphins also happens when you think. Thinkers who feel they are on form and are thinking clearly, have what they call 'flow'. Another way of describing this is as a cross between mental agility and momentum – the ability to operate a series of mental tipping points. Imagine how a Rubik's Cube turns from chaotic mixtures of colours to order in your hands and you get the idea.

You can learn how to think like this and you're going to like it.

Our brain is growing not dying (if we choose)

Most depressing of all for me when I started researching this book was the realisation that no one still really knows that much about how the brain works (except this, which I rather like: compared to the human brain the computer is as mundane as a can-opener). But the computer brain plus a human's brain, well that's another story. The human problem is this: we're told that our brain cells are dying off at the rate of knots. So as I sit here writing this those little blighters are lining up at the mental crematorium in droves. That's why my writing could in theory get worse and worse as time passes. Worse and worse ...

But here's the good news. Our brains can actually grow too. Research shows that taxi drivers' brains grow as they do 'The Knowledge' – yes, the hippocampus actually gets bigger. The same is true with violinists where the part of the brain that operates the nimble fingers of their left hand, grows. Ditto ice skaters and their sense of balance.[5]

It gets better. There's strong evidence that as you get older you can get actually more creative.

And writers can write better and better.[6]

The bottom line is simply this. You can train your brain.

And it's about time we all started so when people ask us 'what do you think?', what comes out of our mouths is a considered, thoughtful and useful reply that people listen to and think about themselves.

Notes

1 A new smartphone app has been developed – 'Spritz' – which increases your reading speed fourfold by firing words at you very fast and cutting out the 80 per cent of the time we waste in reading which is in moving our eyes. Now you see I like moving my eyes... it's part of the fun. Next they'll introduce 'Gulp' an app that helps you get through the tedium of meals where 80 per cent of the time is wasted chewing.

2 Rory Sutherland is Deputy Chair of the Ogilvie Group. He speaks on TED and writes for the *Spectator* magazine. He is an engaging think-outside-the-box thinker who, amongst other things, advocates hiring people with poor degrees (they're likely to have led much more interesting and fun lives at university) and eschewing expensive high-speed transport schemes for ones which cost less to build and are slower but where fine wine is served by good

looking boys and girls by way of compensation. It's less expensive to provide and more fun for the consumer.

3   The Myers-Briggs Type Indicator(MBTI) assessment is a psychometric questionnaire designed to measure psychological preferences in how people make decisions. These preferences were extrapolated from the typological theories of Jung. He theorised that there are four principal psychological functions by which we experience the world: sensation, intuition, feeling, and thinking. The original developers of the personality inventory were Katharine Cook Briggs and her daughter, Isabel Briggs Myers. I am not a fan.

4   William of Occam was a 14th century philosopher whose thinking stated simplicity of causality was a sound principle. Later philosophers acknowledged this broad principle of avoiding complexity and whilst there is no scientific basis to it, it remains a useful, pragmatic rule of thumb. William is just very sensible.

5   Carol Dwek is Professor of Psychology at Stanford University. Her book *Mindset* about exploring motivations is regarded as seminal, is good on this and talks persuasively about fixed and growth mindsets. We need the latter if we are to really grow our skills. As she says of people with 'growth mindsets': 'They don't necessarily think everyone's the same or anyone can be Einstein, but they believe everyone can get smarter if they work at it.'

6   Hilary Mantel is in her 60s; Donna Leon in her 70s; Daniel Kahneman in his 80s; and P.D. James in her 90s.

PART 1

How to use your most important asset – your brain

We have the choice of revitalising our thinking. We can train our brain to work better and harder. We can learn to think more clearly. The trouble is no one has bothered to explain why we aren't thinking well and how we can change this. What follows should be useful food for thought.

CHAPTER 1

Your thinking machine needs looking after

Why thinking has stopped

That would be an exaggeration. We haven't stopped thinking. But the process of thinking in business has become problematic. Senior executives like Ian Parker, CEO of insurer Equity Red Star, describe the difficulty of stopping to think when the machine he's running is moving so fast with so many parts whirring at once. Others blame the US style of management where quantity and pace of activity wins over quality of thinking and where stopping to think is seen as akin to stopping work.

Recent research into investment banks shows 50 per cent of the time executives spend on their PCs at work is on non-work related activity. And we can be sure it's not being spent on thinking. Quite simply there's too much noise, distraction and new stuff happening on the screens in front of us to do more than react to it.

Open-plan offices don't help. They're good for osmosis and spreading germs but they are bad for concentration. It's so easy to fire off half-thought-through e-mails and then spend hours repairing the damage these have created. It's really hard not to reply at once but if you do that you will interrupt the flow of whatever it was you were and should have been thinking about.

In my experience most executives feel tyrannised by their technology, e-mails, texts and voicemails. They have to be online or they feel short-changed. All this is impeding our ability to think and we've got to stop it. Worst of all is the obsession with multi-tasking. Someone described in awe how their teenage children could text, watch TV, look at Google and do their homework simultaneously. But they can't. Ask any neuroscientist. They are doing each quite badly compared to what they should be doing and they are definitely not thinking. It can't be done.

Rachel Bell, Chairman and CEO of Shine Communications, is adamant that she will never multitask. She says she works very fast but applies 100 per cent of her mind to each task she's doing consecutively and never tries to do them concurrently.

 **tip**

> Don't multitask, it stops you thinking properly.

Thinking doesn't feed that primal urge in business – the need to look busy and to feel busy. This red-meat feeling of rushing into a meeting making an impact, scoring some goals, sending some e-mails and then rushing off to another meeting while operating, always, on the bizarre notion that it's great to be late.

Unless we start to change the way we operate we'll never be any great shakes as a thinker and we'll only ever be reactive rather than proactive.

How to start thinking again

We'll give ourselves the best chance to think brilliantly by being in a good mood. There was an historic view that creativity is best achieved when we're in pain and suffering. It's the '*La Bohème*, freezing hand in a freezing garret' concept. And it's nonsense. You think better when you feel well, when you feel happy, when you feel good about yourself and your surroundings.

Our self-esteem is fragile. Amy Chua who earned some notoriety with her book *Battle Hymn of the Tiger Mother* has identified the characteristics of success as self-confidence spiced by self-doubt and overlaid with an obsession to do well. Being self-confident is how we want to be perceived and when we are, our self-esteem rises accordingly. In that state our brain always seems to operate better.

We also need to be in the right place. Never underestimate the benefits and importance of a place that's warm, quiet and pleasant. Nancy Kline, who wrote the book *Time to Think*, which shows above all how to listen brilliantly and in so doing how to generate thinking at unusually powerful levels, is passionate about environment. 'Create the right environment and people will think for themselves,' she says.

For others like banker Paul Zisman, walking is the activity which helps clear the brain and allow concentrated thought. I find that by getting out and looking at things like shop fronts, posters, people's faces and making the subject of my thoughts real, I can start to think more clearly.

 **tip**

You'll think best in the place and in the mood that makes you most alert and relaxed at the same time. Call it a state of 'quiet and active curiosity'.

When thinking, we should use our senses, not just sit there mutely hoping a thought will crop up. Imagine thinking about how to market a whisky. We should touch the bottle, smell the liquid, taste it, look at it on the shelf and listen to what people say about it.

And then we create momentum in our thinking by, as it were, changing the rules. Try looking at things again from a different angle. For example if that bottle of whisky were a bottle of wine or a box of fine cigars or a sports car how might we think about it then? I call this glancing at a problem sideways in an attempt to re-orientate the problem we face.

An experiment was done to see the effect of role playing. Respondents were asked to imagine they were either a university professor or a football hooligan doing an intelligence test. The results were true to the stereotypes. University professors 5: football hooligans 1. Just by thinking themselves into the role of a football hooligan respondents became blokeish and less bright thinking. Try it yourself. Chant 'zigger, zagger, zigger, zagger, oy, oy, oy' three times and your IQ takes a dive.

Unblocking your brains

You need to remove anything which annoys you, distracts you or diverts your interest. Go back to what we know about that brain of ours. It's easily put off and it's inclined to be a bit lazy. This is not a machine, it's a living mind with a memory bank that's amazing but deep down it has a low boredom threshold. And here are three things designed to block it:

- **Task shifting** – the extreme form of multitasking that destroys our ability to think properly although not always to do simple tasks. There you are, busy thinking about how to create a document or whatever and someone walks in and says: 'Can you check that appraisal you did for Maisie. I think it's going to cause us problems.' The sirens go off. You drop what you're doing and Maisie gets your attention. When you get back to your document your mind is no longer on it. Thinking blocked.

- **Time pressure** – stress makes us brain-frozen and unable to think clearly. When someone says 'I need this now' we are unable to say 'no' or 'sorry it takes longer than now'. So we do a poor job, get stressed and probably, as we present it,

are told by the person who's demanded it 'now': 'Thanks –
fine… I'll look at it tomorrow.' Thinking blocked. Probably
blocked for the rest of the day.

- **Imposing self-control** – research shows this uses up a lot
  of brain-space and is hugely effortful. I was surprised by
  Daniel Kahneman's[1] work which showed being diplomatic,
  restraining the impulse to argue or remonstrate creates a
  great deal of mental activity. It's as if we were discovering
  that mental braking uses more fuel than accelerating.
  Self-control blocks thinking. And this means that in many
  meetings there's very little chance of getting people to think
  deeply as they grind their teeth frustrated by the normal
  tedium of long agendas.

 **tip**

Get rid of the thinking blocks one by one and feel the difference.

The role for data in our theatrical brains

I may seem to be overly dramatic in depicting our brains as
places of theatre with actors strutting their stuff. Certainly
psychologists may look askance at my tendency to use a 'homun-
culus' (anthropomorphising a little man in our heads) as a way
of trying to describe what is going on in our minds. But I see the
brain as something of a theatre with various plays being acted
out. One hopes they'll be more like Tom Stoppard and high-
brow comedy than Ben Travers and farce. Whichever way, our
brains are driven by intuition which means most of the thinking
we do happens backstage in our unconscious.

It also means that opinion matters more or generally plays a
bigger role in our thinking than data. The work done on 'fast
thinking' and the experiments cited in Malcolm Gladwell's[2]

book *Blink* show we have well trained instincts. And there's evidence that this starts early in our lives. In research, when we get people to instantly categorise faces – nice or nasty, trustworthy or devious – giving them exposure to these faces, shown to them in rapid succession for just a tenth of a second each, then even three-year-olds do well at it.

But there's a downside to this speed of response. Once we've made our minds up about something, once we've decided, we find it very hard to change our minds. This means it's a good idea to delay making a decision for as long as possible and to consult as many relevant people as possible about our prospective decision. We simply need to give our unconscious time to process all the information we have.

 **tip**

Delay making a decision as long as possible.

And we need especially to review data. In their recent book, *Big Data*, Kenneth Cukier and Viktor Mayer-Schönberger[3] tell the story of a world changed from carefully recruited samples of say 2000 where, in other words, $n = 2000$ to a world where $n =$ all. They describe a thinking change from executives puzzling about 'why' something happens to 'what' happens when something else happens. 'If we change our policy from x to y what happens to our share of votes?' matters more to politicians rather than caring about the causality of the behaviour change. 'I'd rather win votes than be a psephologist,' I can hear them say.

Bringing the data story to brilliant life was done in the Brad Pitt film *Moneyballs*. This the true story about the baseball team, the Oakland Raiders, and how General Manager, Billy Beane, together with Yale economist, Peter Brand, build a team by recruiting players not on their looking the part but on a detailed analysis of their on-field performance. Scouts walk out in disgust as players they don't like the look of make up what they predict will be a joke team. The joke, ultimately, is that the Oakland Raiders win 20 consecutive games, an American League record. The method is called 'sabermetrics' and it was the start of how data trounced instinct in baseball and thereafter in other sports. What data cannot tell you however is the mental make-up of a player at a given moment and what's going on in his or her mind, which, in its turn, also trounces data.

Using data well is a skill you need to work on. I was recently told to avoid using averages like the plague. Puzzled I asked why. Because on average the UK population has one testicle and one breast I was told. And what use is that as a piece of information?

Great data matters and has never been more accessible or useful.

brilliant tip

Create an alliance between a good thinker and a great set of data and you have an unbeatable team.

'Don't believe a word of it'

Never take anything for granted. It's too easy to nod and say 'yes' but the art of asking 'why' and the willingness to say 'no' mark out a thinker. Theodore Sturgeon,[4] Sci-Fi writer, on being told 90 per cent of Sci-Fi writing was crap said, '90 per cent of everything is crap'. He was thinking of all forms of product and he was probably right. This has a certain appeal and became known as Sturgeon's Law. Another (but, I think, better) thing he said was: 'Nothing is always absolutely so.'

The ability to ask that killer question – Why? – is what distinguishes the effective executive. Recently I came across a situation where I watched a board of directors sleepwalk its way into a decision that was expedient, easy to get agreed and just plain wrong. The only child (as opposed to an elephant in the room) who asked the 'why isn't the Emperor wearing any clothes?' question got short shrift but the doubt he created hung over the board like a bad smell. I think they remembered what Bertrand Russell said:

> 'The trouble with the world is that the stupid are cocksure and the intelligent are full of doubt.'

Always question everything to avoid gravitation to the accepted myths of life. Keep on asking 'why?' until you get a good answer. Keep wondering why the people whom you are questioning say what they are saying. Try to get them to think about it.

Time for lunch

You think I'm being frivolous? I spent many years in advertising where the thoughtful conversations over lunch were often the most productive things I did during a working day. For me Michelin food and 'brain food' went together.

Yet I hadn't realised how right I was. Some 25 per cent of the calories we consume every day are required by the 1.5kg of neural tissue that's our brain and it also snatches 75 per cent of the glucose we consume. Our brain is a 'gas guzzler' so to keep it running well we really need to eat plenty.

Ever since Michael Douglas as Gordon Gekko in the film *Wall Street* said 'Lunch? Aw, you gotta be kidding. Lunch is for wimps', lunch has gone out of favour in business. Gekko also said that 'The most valuable commodity I know of... is information.' And more people get more information over lunch than they ever do sitting at their desks.

 **tip**

A good lunch helps you think.

Over a lunch table information tumbles out. So don't diet yourself to demotion. The weight problem you should really be worrying about is mental obesity. David Ryan Polgar, author of *Wisdom in the Age of Twitter*, said this is our biggest thinking issue because 'we binge on junk information'. He goes on:

'A healthy digital lifestyle is about finding a balance between information consumption and reflection, which allows the information to move to a higher level of thinking. A healthy digital lifestyle consists of less data, better information, more reflection, and mental exercise.'

And lunch, David. And lunch.

Think of work as being like tennis

When people say there's no time to think, and the list of people who said this to me is a long one, and that there are too many moving parts to be operated to sit down for a second, just remember action-packed tennis.

Let's get this in perspective. At the top level, in a typical three-set match where the score is 6–4, 6–4, 6–4 players will sprint over 3 miles, facing serves in excess of 150 mph. Yet the players will get to sit by the umpire (with their towels) and think for around 25 minutes during that match.

Can't you spend the same sort of time at work – say 1½ hours of your working day – just sitting and thinking (the towel is optional)?

 **tip**

The break between games is when you think.

Release that Einstein inside you

We really are better at this than we think we are. But we are especially lacking in confidence when it comes to creative thinking. This is because we imagine being creative means being quirky. Pink sheep, jokes no one understands and long silences. Consider Rap + Post Modern Art + Noh Theatre + Street Dance + 4.33 (John Cage's silent concerto) and you have the kind of creativity that would have most sane people running for the drinks cabinet.

Yet in business our entry point for creative thinking is actually simple. We have to start by asking 'how can we make this better?' US ad man Ed McCabe put it beautifully when, representing the whole of the creative body in advertising, he said: 'There's nothing new under the sun but there's always a better way.'

Creativity is when you're bubbling over with lots of thoughts. Getting to that frame of mind is relatively easy if you follow a series of techniques. What creativity is not, although some may try to persuade you otherwise, is random. Above all it is a disciplined process.

Why packaging your thinking matters

Daniel Kahneman describes an experiment designed to baffle rational thinking economists in which people elected a strong preference for a financial reward enclosed in a 'big, blue envelope' as opposed to just getting the cash. This does not compute, as Mr Spock might say. Yet the respondents who said they preferred the idea said that it sounded like a celebration and hoped there might even be a party.

 **tip**

> How you present and package your thinking distinguishes thinking from great thoughts.

To anyone in marketing this is all great news. Because it means consumers like you to market your thinking and dress it up, not just let your thought escape like a moment of mental flatulence. There's another aspect to this as well. Working out how to present your thinking at its best forces you to get the thoughts to be clear, simple and compelling.

Jack Welch, the legendary CEO of General Electric, said: 'I always thought that chart-making clarified my thinking better than anything else.'

Remember, thinking has to be well expressed to be well received.

The four kinds of thinking

These are most useful in business, when they are mastered, to enable you to achieve your best at work. Welcome to critical thinking, decision-making thinking, creative thinking and empathetic thinking (being able to understand how and why others think the way they do and thinking about how best to work with them).These are our ways of winning in the business of out-thinking others.

Notes

1   Daniel Kahneman is a psychologist and winner of the 2002 Nobel Memorial Prize in Economic Sciences. Famed for his work on the psychology of judgment and decision-making, behavioural economics and hedonic psychology he wrote *Thinking Fast, Thinking Slow* in 2011 and at the age of 80 is in heavy demand as a speaker. He's regarded as one of the world's most important thinkers. Hope for us all as we get older.

2   Malcolm Gladwell is an American journalist and best-selling author of a series of highly readable and seminal books – *Tipping Point*, *Blink*, *The Outliers*, *What the Dog Saw* and *David and Goliath*.

3   *Big Data: A Revolution that Will Transform How We Live, Work and Think* is an important exposé and revelatory exploration of the hottest trend in technology and the dramatic impact it will have on the economy, science, and society at large. Cukier is the Data Editor of the *Economist* and Mayer-Schönberger is Professor of Internet Governance and Regulation at Oxford University.

4   Theodore Sturgeon (1918–85) was an American science fiction and horror writer and critic. His most famous book was *More Than Human*.

PART 2

Summary: brilliant thinking on a plate

One of the big issues in the modern world is shortage of time. We all seem to be too busy. Arguably a book of a few hundred pages suggesting how to think more effectively simply adds to the pressure on your time. That's why this part is the 'ready prepared thinking meal'. If you only read this you'll get the essence of the story I have to tell. It'll be the instruction leaflet rather than the manual but hopefully it'll be a lot better than nothing.

CHAPTER 2

A brilliant thinking toolkit

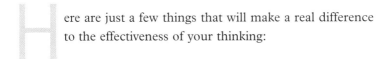

ere are just a few things that will make a real difference to the effectiveness of your thinking:

1. How to think more brilliantly

Balance your opinions and your rational arguments

Our minds have two thinking systems. The intuitive 'how I feel' part and the rational 'I'm thinking through the facts' part. We need to get both working together rather than just either part (and it's usually our opinion part that's strongest) driving our thinking. Be aware of what you feel and what you know. Balance your opinion against the facts. Keep on questioning. Control your impulses.

Find the thinking stimuli that work for you

Daniel Dennett[1] put it well when he noted you couldn't do much carpentry with your bare hands. So what makes you think you can do much useful thinking with your bare brain? The misconception is that we think that by impersonating Rodin's thinker in a dramatic, reflective pose we'll look the part and therefore be the part. We're thinking, of course, the whole time. But the concentrated thinking that makes the real day-to-day difference is done by exploiting tools and stratagems which vary from going for a walk to sitting to reading a book on the subject to looking at the product we're thinking about (not glancing but really looking at it) to going and listening to some consumers talking about it, really listening, actively listening to them. Use whatever tools you can find to feed your mind and clear your head, from the chisel of consumer research to the hammer of using the product again and again and again, and really getting to know it.

Think properly by not doing something else at the same time

Do not multitask because it stops you focusing. Focus is going to be a very well-used word in this book. If you were reading a book on tennis the author would probably find it unnecessary to say 'watch the ball' but in business 'keep your focus and concentration on the problem' cannot be said enough. And you know, by now, my attitude to multitasking. Hung, drawn and quartered, and then some, is the penalty for that.

Defend what you've got before you try to acquire more

All the research done by psychologists tells us that humans are much more upset by losing something than they are excited by gaining something. In golf the percentage of putts made to save par successfully are significantly greater than the percentage made to make a successful birdie. On the basis that people in business are in fact humans, think how this has an impact on the way they work through problems and decisions. Remember that colleagues of yours, whether they consciously realise it or not, do not want to lose what they have gained so far. That is their red line. Try it with salaries. Which provokes the more dramatic effect: 'come in... we've decided to increase your salary' or 'come in... we've decided to reduce your salary'? Rage at loss will beat pleasure from gain.

Think out loud to form your thoughts

Nancy Kline[2] in *Time to think* is strongly supportive of people talking about their thoughts as they form in their minds to an attentive and supportive listener who doesn't interrupt. When somebody listens that actively, your thoughts tumble out uncensored but build one on another. Incisive questions like 'tell me what you really think' sometimes provoke the most extraordinarily descriptive and profound answers.

2. How to use your thinking time better

Take your time

We tend to rush our thinking and it suffers when we do. It's the action packed atmosphere of business today which makes us want to seem decisive (but this often seems impulsive), articulate (but this often seems glib and gabby) and well briefed (but this often seems Wikipedia lightweight). I recall someone some years ago telling me about being in a room with all the heavyweight senior grocery retailers discussing the economy. The person who spoke last, doing so quietly and with authority, was Terry Leahy of Tesco. Everyone hung on his every word. Take your time, get your thoughts in order and think what the best thing to say is – and then keep it simple.

Stop being so busy – it's a state of mind

Chaucer ironically describes a lawyer in his poem *The Canterbury Tales* as always seeming busier than he was. Over 500 years ago this sharp witted and funny man teasing the preposterous man of business for rushing around like the Rabbit in *Alice in Wonderland* puffing 'oh my ears and whiskers' and pretending he was important, remains in my mind as a shrewd observer of how we all are. It's still fashionable to be busy. But it's also cool to be a bit laid-back. And remember the smart money is on the thoughtful. But pause… that's not always possible, so think about it. Here's what authors of *Nudge*,[3] a highly influential book suggest: 'Busy people are trying to cope in a complex world in which they cannot afford to think deeply about every choice they make.' So relax a bit and don't look flustered.

Think about how to think more loosely

Sociologist William Cameron[4] memorably said: 'Not everything that counts can be counted, and not everything that can be counted counts.' We live in an age of targets, of things being measured and, whilst nothing I'm going to say will change that, I can help us think beyond a breathlessly achieved number and help us move to the next level. We can loosen up and be a bit more creative. Apart from anything else it's more fun and makes going to work much more interesting. The urge to reduce every-thing to a number is decried in a book called *The Tyranny of Numbers* by John Seddon, an occupational psychologist special-ising in the public sector and service industries. Personally I'm with Don Norman,[5] the designer, who said: 'If it's too simple it gets boring.' Yes Don. It does.

Slow down – reduce stress levels

I was running a meeting and for some reason the 'one-man-band' trap engulfed me. I found myself pouring the coffee, moving the chairs, doing the introductions; in effect, doing everything. The effects of this were that I got puffed, flustered and paranoid. Whether Deidre had sugar in her coffee suddenly seemed as critical as whether the charity had enough money to carry on with its current project. I was stressed. And to be honest I stopped paying attention and my critical thinking faculty just shut down. Advice: slow down. Ask others to help. Set up things really painstakingly before accelerating. Distinguish between two needs: pouring coffee slowly and quickly gauging the mood of people and any issues you sense might be brewing up. And remember anyone can pour the coffee.

Doing nothing may be a positive action

It may seem a good, positive act to make a decision when you actually really don't have to. It calls for courage to say, 'We don't know enough and this isn't urgent enough to rush into. Let's get more information, think some more and then we'll try again.' There's a story in Apple of the launch of the first Apple Store being delayed because it just wasn't quite right yet. In politics, decisions are parked because a consensus can't be reached. That's how democracy works.

Turn off, let your unconscious take over

We have an automatic pilot which they call the 'adaptive unconscious'. This is what gets us to work safely and on time when we honestly can't remember doing the journey. When you walk down the crowded pavement thinking about a meeting how come you don't have more head-on crashes with other people? Your adaptive unconscious is to thank for that as it is for letting you smell danger, do what needs doing and for helping you simply size up things. Trust it. It's impressive. And then there's your intuition that's shaping your thoughts as you walk, talk, eat and sleep. I'm tempted to say this book was written almost entirely in my sleep which would make my point (but it wasn't – writing is a pretty sleepless business in fact). Trust your unconscious mind but also give it the tools and data it craves.

3. How to behave to help others think

Say 'I don't know' when you don't know

In ancient times there was strong evidence of the mental skill traders had in bartering by mentally gauging. Foreign exchange was done not on the screen but in the head. In psychological terms, 'anchoring', which means having reference points, can be a useful gauging tool but it can also be very misleading. Ask me how many people are in a theatre and I anchor my perception to what a school assembly of 500 looks like. But if the audience is 2000 I'm less sure-footed. Ask most women (my wife for instance) and they'll simply say, 'I don't know.' I now believe we'd all be a lot better off saying 'I don't know' more often and getting someone to find out… properly – not sloppily on Google or Wikipedia.

Think in relation to the real situation you're in

We behave differently if we know the context in which something occurs. If I say 'he choked on…' without you knowing what follows, it could be either:

- a piece of rare steak, or
- seeing he had a two foot putt to win the match.

You won't know how to react. The probable response will be very different, between, for instance, 'How do you do the Heimlich manoeuvre and save his life?' or, if he's my opponent in this important golf match, 'How can I discreetly gloat without it being too obvious?' We must know where, when, how and why the issue we are thinking about occurs. We must consider if it's a stand-alone, unique happening or something related to previous events. We'll view an action replay differently, for instance, using lots of hindsight than we will when we see something for the first time.

Don't interrupt people

I confess I was a terrible interrupter until I started to study this phenomenon. My father used to say there was no point in trying to interrupt because all too often the moment had gone when an intercession really worked as a constructive addition to the conversation. But I'd spent my life wanting to get MY point across. No more. I'm on a self-imposed programme of letting thoughts build and people having their heads. Good chairmen and women are those who let the meeting create something useful, who are facilitators and not dictators.

Have more than one option in making a decision

Things have moved on. No one has just one option to offer now. There is always more than one solution. The tempestuous thinker

Nassim Nicholas Taleb,[6] *The Black Swan* author, is (rightly) contemptuous of the 'one-dish-on-the menu' approach saying:

'A decision without an alternative is a desperate gambler's throw.'

Trying to sell a one option choice is frankly not selling at all; it's coercion. Yet the issue is one of sensible choice offering, say, three options to see which suits you best. This is manageable and not the stressful choice you get in a large supermarket. Waitrose, for example, offers 348 cheese options online. Research at Bristol University shows 47 per cent of people in a survey stayed awake at night stressed by the choices they had to make. I doubt if they're thinking about cheese but who knows.

But quite simply a decision without a choice of options is not a decision.

Look at things with a wide-angled lens

We look at things too often through a microscope seeing the detail and missing the big picture or, alternatively, like an 18th century general looking through an eyeglass from the top of a hill whence through cannon smoke and confusion he can't really see what's going on. You're either too near or too far away. You see all trees or all wood. Neither perspective really works. Instead think about using a wide-angled lens which gives you a broad view of what's going on. Think about things from a variety of points of view – from a historical perspective, a geographical perspective, an employee perspective, a customer perspective, an economic perspective or a broader stakeholder perspective.

Mayer-Schönberger and Kenneth Cukier, the *Big Data* authors, get the perspective thing spot-on when they say: 'You need a broad idea of what's going on to make an informed decision.' Broad ideas are what we all need.

By way of shaking up his team I heard of a CEO recently who asked people to look at things through the perspective of doing the job really badly, being awful at every facet, on the basis that this was a short cut to seeing how to do it really well.

Another CEO, before making a really expensive investment decision, gets his team to do a pre-mortem:

'Imagine that it's five years on and this has been a catastrophe… what went wrong and could we have foreseen it?'

And another who always asks his team to see things from a competitor's viewpoint:

'What would you think and, more importantly, what would you do if you were our biggest competitor?'

Synchronise how you think with how others think

Or for short 'sync-think'. At the heart of any thinking organisation exists not that awful word 'alignment' which always reminds me of Nazi Germany but the synchronisation you see in a great team working and thinking together, anticipating, reacting, sharing and executing. Go into any restaurant on form and you'll see this in action. My favourite book on management is not what you might expect. It's Anthony Bourdain's *Les Halles Cookbook*.[7] In it he describes running a kitchen so vividly you feel its pulse and the process of learning to be a cook:

'Eventually, your hands, your palate, even your ears will learn, they will know in advance when things are in danger of going wrong.'

In today's working-together world where wild eccentric loners have a tough time learning to synchronise their thinking with others, they'll learn the best way of doing this is by listening to and watching what others do.

4. Get your attitude of mind right for thinking brilliantly

Where you think changes how well you do it

Marcus Alexander is the Professor of Strategy and Entrepreneurship at the London Business School. He's a very smart, knowledgeable, clear thinker. He says you've got to get your thinking space right, the lighting, the quiet, the chair, the atmosphere – he says it really matters. Yet some of us work and do our thinking in what, were it clothing as opposed to ergonomics we're talking about, would make us look like 1930s tramps.

Plants help, your own desk as opposed to a hot desk works… imagine 'hot clothes' – sharing shoes and trousers… nice (not). And sometimes a bit of mess works – so long as it's your mess. As Einstein said:

'If a cluttered desk is a sign of a cluttered mind, of what, then, is an empty desk a sign?'

Being in a good mood matters even more

It's fairly obvious that we work better when we are in a good mood but that doesn't mean a bit of edge and adrenalin doesn't help. Enoch Powell[8] used to speak in the House of Commons on a full bladder to create a frisson of excitement. But that's just weird. Don't even think about it. The feeling of being at one with yourself, your subject and feeling comfortable in your shoes creates what is called 'cognitive ease'. Being in a state of mind where we feel nimble witted and focused on what we want to achieve rather than grumbling about the potholes on the journey on the way to the meeting seems perfect. It's when you watch Sir Kenneth Robinson[9] talk when he's on song, that you see that cognitive ease at its lubricious best. Emile Zola put it beautifully when he said: 'I am here to live out loud.'

Care less about what others think of you

Lucy Kellaway, who writes for the *Financial Times*, told of when she was cycling nervously on her way to make a talk. (Nervously because of the stage fright a presentation gives many, stage-fright because of what others may think of us.) She was nearly killed as someone opened their car door and she had to swerve, narrowly avoiding a head on collision with a van. And during all this dice-with-death she felt calm, controlled and slightly irritated.

She thought about it and realised how crazy this was. After all, she was going to talk to some civilised people about a subject she knew, in a nice environment and she faced this prospect with less equanimity than death.

We worry what people thought about what we wore (they didn't notice), what we said (they didn't hear) and what a cock up we made (they didn't remember).

We become incapable of thinking about the stuff that really matters because we worry about a wine stain on our shirt.

Stop being so vain… it's what you think that matters not what you think others think of you.

Look for truth in people's faces

When you put your hand over a baby's hand the baby doesn't look at the hand over theirs, instead they look at your face for the answer.

An investor like Nicola Horlick[10] says she wants to meet the CEO of a business she's invested in so 'she can see the whites of his eyes'.

'The one-tenth of a second do you trust this person?' test is of people's faces not of anything else; just their faces. Ten glimpses of different faces in just one second is enough for us to know whether the person is a rotter or a good guy.

Malcolm Gladwell[11] writes about Silvan Tompkins, a psychologist who died in 1991 but whose understanding of the 'human face' was legendary. He identified 10,000 different, visible facial configurations and demonstrated he could, as he put it, 'unpack the face' to decode whether people were telling the truth but more than that... what they were actually thinking about as opposed to what they were saying.

Be more relaxed about playing and celebrating

I believe we now tend to take life far too seriously.

In French Gold Abbott[12] where I worked, we'd play elaborate games of golf in our offices, insisting on playing the ball where it lay on a PA's desk, test the Evel Knievel toy bike and bet on whether it would make it ramp to ramp. At another agency, FCO, we created a new form of curling, sliding our 'stone', a Bernard Matthews Frozen Leg of Lamb, along a parquet floor with account men armed with brooms sweeping wildly in front of it as it made its uncertain way towards the circular target that they call the 'house'.

Play and celebration, laughter and champagne have played a large part in my life. Some of our best ideas seemed to come after being exceedingly silly. The master of play and celebration in my life was Richard French, an uproarious party giver and a supple creative thinker. Playing and celebration has a purpose – ask the people at Google. Anyone who's visited its European HQ sees focus and fun mixed together. But my guess is without the table football, slides and free food they'd all go insane.

Be an optimist

Because you'll live longer and think better that way.

There's a piece of longitudinal research, I recall, that was done with nuns which compellingly showed optimistic nuns live longer than pessimistic nuns (although that's not really that surprising).

Richard Wiseman[13] who's a Professor of Psychology and a debunker of the paranormal has done interesting work on luck. One of his discoveries shows optimists are simply more likely to get lucky than pessimists.

For instance it's the optimist who finds the £5 note on the floor not the pessimist. He says:

'My research revealed that lucky people generate their own good fortune via four basic principles. They are skilled at creating and noticing chance opportunities, make lucky decisions by listening to their intuition, create self-fulfilling prophesies via positive expectations and adopt a resilient attitude that transforms bad luck into good.'

We discover that almost nothing in life is as important as you think it is when you are thinking about it. Nor do things turn out badly, just differently to our expectations. When you're busy doing project A, a solution to the intractable project B comes to mind. The brain is good at this.

5. Get your thoughts translated into action

Change your mind when things around you change

John Maynard Keynes, the iconic economist, asked: 'When circumstances change I change my mind. What do you do?' But we all of us find it really hard to change our minds. It goes against our psychological grain. Deep down we've invested too much time and effort championing an idea or point of view to lightly discard it.

One of the best tips to help open your mind and broaden your thinking is for you to see how easy it would be for you to change your mind about something you believe in. I recently heard a story about the late William Rees-Mogg, a man with a brilliant mind who was a past editor of *The Times*. He said that a given *Times* leader should say 'x'. When politely told that his grasp of the facts was shaky and that in fact 'y' was the case, he said without pausing for breath, 'Quite so, which is why we must espouse the cause of "y" for the following reasons.' Now that is open-minded, flexible and extraordinarily clever, although some might say cynical.

The human race when it feels informed tends to overconfidence which leads us to nearly all the economic crises we have had. It's overconfidence not greed that's the enemy of the bank balance. We tend to forecast boldly but make timid decisions. Think about this the next time you are sitting in front of your forecast spreadsheet. Most of all think this: 'Does my plan match my hopes, expectations and (most importantly) my resources?' I bet it doesn't.

Make small things matter

Transformative thoughts are very rare. It's the small steps that take us forward. Occasionally a genius emerges and writes *Othello* or paints *The Last Supper* or composes a Requiem Mass which changes the world from being 'in black and white to colour when you hear it' (that's how composer Eric Whitacre described the effect of his first hearing Mozart's *Requiem Mass*). Or someone does something extraordinary in business, at Apple or Pixar or Paramount or Samsung.

But mostly it's the small-step-for-mankind incremental improvement that allows a brick-sized mobile phone to evolve to a watch-sized one and then back again to a tablet-sized one.

'New improved' are the two most thought provoking words in the marketing vocabulary. Think about that as your brief, rather than flying to Mars. Think like Confucius in taking it step by step on your journey of innovation.

Real creativity is creating something useful and exciting to be used now, not being ahead of your time or creating something that doesn't make customers smile with pleasure.

Make your thinking real by using prototypes

Because paper plans are paper planes – that's all they are. When Steve Backley, the one-time world record holder for the javelin, was preparing for the 2000 Olympics in Sydney, he did something pretty serious. He tore a cartilage. It seemed unlikely he'd recover in time or, if he did, that he'd be tournament fit. He described how he got fit in his mind by lying next to the javelin throwing area at various stadiums visualising what it would be like throwing over 90 metres and winning a gold medal. He smelt the grass, he felt the moisture in the turf, he visualised the sound of the crowd, he breathed deep and he visualised. He said it felt like the real thing. So when it came to Sydney he was ready for the experience. This was as near to creating a prototype as a supine athlete can get.

Do not think in strategies which set out the obvious like 'my strategy is to win a gold medal by throwing the javelin further than anyone else'. Instead think your way through the event step by step. Make it real in your head.

The great Edwardian architect Sir Edwin Landseer Lutyens realised how difficult it was for his clients to imagine a design. So when he designed Castle Drogo in Devon for businessman Julius Drewe in the 1920s (the last English castle built only in granite) he realised Julius didn't really get the drawn plans. So he built a full size Castle Drogo façade in wood and drove Julius Drewe in from where the entrance would be so a breathtaking first impression could be achieved.

That's how good prototypes work: so good that they're almost real.

A great thought's a dead thought when people won't buy it

In advertising, I was involved in a lot of competitive pitches for new business assignments. Because a lot of money as well as prestige is at stake, you worked really hard on the presentation.

And you usually came up with a solution which you presented to your prospective client with passion and utter conviction. The philosopher in me always realised that some you win and some you lose but you always hoped you could tilt things your way and beat the odds. However a number of times after wasted hours and a resounding 'thank you but no thank you' from the prospective client I'd hear colleagues say, 'Well if I did it all over again I wouldn't change a thing.'

That, come to think of it, is Einstein's theory of insanity in action; doing the same thing over and over again and expecting different results. The best solution (on paper) may not be one that can be sold internally within a company. We live in a world where you need to sell something to your client so at that point you can start working together. And working together, thinking together is the real goal. Not trying to sell a solution the customer doesn't want.

Don't listen too hard to clever people (they are often wrong)

I was struck by the brilliant degrees in maths or physics that all the creators of collateralised debt obligations had.[14] These were very clever people, as were the marketers who packaged up these CDOs to look their best. Psychological research shows our critical faculties shut down when we consult an expert. This is, I suspect, especially true when left-brain probability theory or anything mathematical or logical is involved.

There's an expression 'too clever for his own good', which applies to people whose expertise clouds their judgement, and the ability to communicate their ideas simply enough for others to understand is non-existent.

The next time someone says 'trust me I'm an expert' – don't. And here's the most telling comment on expertise I know. It's from Warren Buffett:

'I try to buy stock in businesses that are so wonderful that an idiot can run them. Because sooner or later, one will.'

 **recap**

These tools are here to think about and use so as to train your brain. In this messy and complex world we need to keep chiselling away at the myths that businesses unthinkingly accept and the strategies not properly thought out that are often embarked on. It's not through mischief or stupidity that so much thoughtlessness occurs in business, it's because most of us assume we are logical beings rather than inconsistent, erratic and lazy thinkers. If life were an exam there'd be fewer A*s than we'd expect. But we can improve. Just try listening harder, not interrupting, smiling, focusing on fewer things, taking your time and being your own person – not worrying what others think quite so much and never being bamboozled by an expert.

That should be a pretty good start.

Notes

1   Daniel Dennett is an American philosopher, writer and cognitive scientist whose research centres on the philosophy of mind, philosophy of science and philosophy of biology. He is a University Professor at Tufts University. Dennett is referred to as one of the 'Four Horsemen of New Atheism', along with Richard Dawkins, Sam Harris and the late Christopher Hitchens. He is the author of *Intuition Pumps*.

2   Nancy Kline is an American-born author, teacher, coach and public speaker who now lives in England. Her best-selling book *Time to Think* has a folksy style but has compelling content and advice.

3   *Nudge: Improving Decisions about Health, Wealth, and Happiness* by Richard Thaler and Cass Sunstein, respectively Professors

in Behavioral Science and Jurisprudence at the University of Chicago, has been highly influential on government and business leaders. It's about planning and creating 'choice architecture' whereby we make more intelligent choices. Life is not easy. Others can make it easier for us. I buy the title. There are better books around.

4   There's extensive and tiresome debate as to whether this was said by Einstein. Evidence suggests Cameron was more likely.

5   Don Norman is an academic in the field of cognitive science, design and usability engineering and a co-founder and consultant with the Nielsen Norman Group. He is the author of the book *The Design of Everyday Things*.

6   Nassim Taleb is a contrarian. He sets out to shake and shock. And he talks a lot of sense. He is a Lebanese American essayist, scholar and statistician, whose work focuses on problems of randomness, probability and uncertainty. His 2007 book *The Black Swan* was described in a review by the *Sunday Times* as one of the 12 most influential books since World War II.

7   Anthony Michael Bourdain is an American chef, author and television personality and executive chef of the Les Halles, French brasserie restaurants in the USA.

8   Enoch Powell. A brilliant orator, politician, classical scholar, linguist and poet, he served as a Conservative Member of Parliament and as a member of the government. He was a controversial figure on immigration in the 1970s.

9   Sir Kenneth Robinson. English author, acclaimed speaker, and international advisor on education in the arts. He was Director of The Arts in Schools Project and Professor of Arts Education at the University of Warwick (1989–2001). He now lives in the USA and is an acclaimed TED speaker.

10   Nicola Horlick is a British Investment Fund Manager. She has been described as 'Superwoman' in the media for balancing her high-flying finance career with bringing up six children.

11 Malcom Gladwell, journalist and best-selling American author of books like *The Tipping Point*. He's probably one of the most influential thinkers around.

12 French Gold Abbott (FGA). British Advertising Agency founded in the early 1970s at the same time as Saatchi and Saatchi and Boase Massimi Pollitt. All three founders went on to form other successful agencies.

13 Richard Wiseman used to be a magician and is now a self-publicist, broadcaster and Professor of the Public Understanding of Psychology at the University of Hertfordshire.

14 A collateralised debt obligation (CDO) is a bundle of mortgages, bonds or whatever that has an anticipated cash flow as payments are made on them at fixed moments. They were assembled in tranches according to their levels of risk, with the most secure paying the lowest returns. But the marketing trick (and I'd argue the 2008 crash could be called the fault of marketing) was to package the basket of fruit with the best, lowest risk fruit on top and the bad sub-prime mortgage apples on the bottom.

PART 3

Critical
thinking

This is the thinking process that we use to solve problems. When they said 'Houston we have a problem' those critical thinkers at NASA got to work. Our problems are probably a bit more prosaic, a bit simpler, more of the order 'why are our sales down?' and 'what can we do about it?' Day in and day out in a knowledge economy our role is not to do what a computer can do but to do what a computer can't do. Namely sort out what to do when the unexpected happens. Of course there's going to be a certain amount of 'grunt work' (quite a lot actually ever since they didn't replace the other guy working alongside you in your office and now you have to do his work too) but it's when the alarms go off that you'd better be on your mettle.

CHAPTER 3

Problem-solvers of the world get ready

'Hey, our sales are down. What can we do about it?'

This is a fairly typical situation. Everything is going fine. You are in a business that's not really thinking but just sleepwalking its way through the financial year. Everything is on course. There've been no surprises. And then you get that 'Mayday call'. You have a problem. And it means you have to think.

One of my favourite quotes is from the British physicist Lord Rutherford who said:

'We have no money so we shall have to think.'

And what's so special about the kind of critical thinking that you need to solve a problem like this one? It's free. So let's get started.

 **tip**

You've got to define the precise nature of the problem. 'Help!!!' is not a brief.

Creating the 'real' brief

To create a brief and the bare bones of a plan there's a simple five-point process that acts as a useful framework but here is one big bold caveat.

> It's critical you don't prejudge anything. Do not decide anything too fast. Use your brain not your opinion at this stage. You are supposed to be thinking... not to have made up your mind.

The five-part thinking process

1. Putting the problem into context

You need information. When did the signs of a sales fall-off first emerge? Is it specific to certain sectors or is it across the board? What's happening to the market as a whole? Are your competitors in the same boat as you or are some of them doing better than others? What's happening with your trade customers? Are some doing better or is this a general malaise? Critically, what's happening to trade stocks? Is there any broader economic story that might provoke a cool down in retailer purchasing? You need shapes, trends and broad numbers not masses of data. At this stage a snapshot of what's been happening rather than a full length video is going to be enough, or should be enough, to get the overall, broad picture.

2. Observation, experience and knowledge

- **Observation.** Do some store trips so you can look at your and your competitors' products as they appear on retailers' shelves. What does this tell you? Maybe not much at this stage but it's focusing your thoughts on the simple reality of your world. You make something. You put it in a box. You ship it to a shop. It sits there till someone buys it (or not). Observation is with the eyes, obviously, but also the ears.

Listen to shoppers. Listen to retailers. Listen to people in your business. Check whether there is any 'oh by the way' discontinuity like – 'oh we changed the recipe recently' or 'there was a price increase six months ago' or 'we changed the way we took orders' or 'we're three salesmen light'… anything.

- **Experience.** The most precious asset and the most dangerous one. It's dangerous as just because 'x' happened before or we did 'y' and it worked, it doesn't mean it's going to be right this time. What psychologists call the 'availability heuristic' namely a 'rule of thumb related to what's available in our minds through our experience' is a double-edged sword. It's great to be familiar with the situation in broad terms but very bad to be drawn into thinking it resembles previous experiences when it may or may not do so. Use experience like seasoning – to sharpen the taste of our observations not to make up the dish as a whole.

- **Knowledge.** I've never encountered a situation where deep knowledge wasn't helpful. I'm not talking about being an expert (you know what I think about experts). I'm talking about the been-there-seen-that-understand-how-things-work-when-you-pull-different-levers kind of knowledge. I'm talking about the knowledge of a craftsman rather than the knowledge of an academic.

The one thing that we, as businesspeople, are truly shocking at is listening to the people in the front line, asking them 'what do you think?', when doing so could save days or weeks and thousands or even millions of pounds.

 **tip**

Ask people who are most immediately affected by the problem 'what do you think?'

These are often the people who really have the knowledge. And you don't need expensive meetings to unlock this – an e-mail or text message can give you invaluable insights of the 'I was actually there and I saw and heard…' sort.

3. Reasoning what's happening, why it's happening and what you can do

Use what you actually know. Academics create a shorthand for this: WYSIATI (what you see is all there is). Avoid speculative theories.

 **tip**

For real thinking to flourish look at the facts first.

Evidence only counts when you can preface it with 'we know that' rather than 'I think that'. Maria Konnikova[1] in *Mastermind* notes that we find it really difficult to pay attention and that our mental default mode is wandering about a bit like a dog in a park where there are lots of interesting smells. Now it's time to stop the curious intuitive tail from wagging the rational dog. It's time to think rationally and forensically. It's time to work out from the facts what's going on. We also need to know why it's going on so we can do something about it. But (and this is really important) finding out *why* it's going on is much less important than discovering *what* you can do to change it.

Beware these thinking snares. They are typical obstacles to thinking with an open mind which sadly we use all the time:

- **Simplifying.** The mind likes simplifying – time for that later – don't edit too soon when you can't see what's good and what's redundant.

- **Seeking big concrete reasons.** Just because these possible reasons don't make themselves clear don't assume they are hidden. Maybe they just don't exist. Maybe there's a mixture of small reasons not one big, solid one.

- **Wanting exciting stories.** The J.K. Rowling in our souls wants to find a Voldemort or a Death Eater or a quest. Best of all we want a conspiracy theory ('Martindale, whom we fired last year for performance reasons, has joined Sizzling Sausages and has spread a whispering campaign about us – it's pure sedition but it's resulted in a sales fall-off. He's out to get us').

- **Insisting on logic and things that make sense.** We want neat, tidy diagnoses. When we go to the doctor we don't want to hear 'I'm not sure but it's probably a slight dose of valetudinarian flu – take a couple of Ibuprofen, cut out alcohol and have an early night. You should feel better in a day or so.' (For me this is when 'man-flu' is likely to kick in, in a very big way and for me to start feeling very sorry for myself.)

4. Deciding 'what to do' – a list of options

This part of the process is where Nobel Prize winning physicist Richard Feynman said real 'scientific imagination' takes place. This is when questions get asked of the preliminary conclusions deriving from the evidence like 'is that really so?' or 'why might that be?' and 'what if?' It's what he calls 'imagination in a tight straitjacket'.

Typically this when a group of people are more likely to generate ideas that are useful, especially if the session is conducted in an anything-goes-relaxed-we'll-harvest-the-good-stuff-later-on spirit.

This is where the thinking really starts.

5. Creating a detailed 'how-to', 'who to' and 'how to track/ measure' action plan

The how-to plan that we need should be a tribute to step-by-step project management not a loose mission statement. To work it requires single point accountability (in other words, for each task and each project someone is nominated or volunteered to be responsible). No one gets off the hook. No one can think they're a mere spectator.

 **tip**

In planning there must be total clarity as to who does what.

Finally the targets need to be precise, actionable and follow a time line, and they must be measurable and measured.

But... however good the thinking, however good the investigation and diagnosis and however inspiring the ideas to restore the sales fortunes of your business, nearly all the emphasis lies on the execution if they are to be of any use.

Thinkers who don't do stuff are worse than being unhelpful, they're just academic spectators who get in the way of progress. William James,[2] the psychologist, put such people in their place: 'A great many people think they are thinking when they are merely rearranging their prejudices.' He also said 'thinking is for doing'. (Although there's some disagreement as to whether these were his exact words. But they'll do, expressing as they do the pragmatism we require from critical thinking.)

Setting ourselves up

Get yourself in the right frame of mind

Extensive research shows we can condition ourselves to be better or worse at thinking. Being in a good mood is the best place to be. Yet, picture the scene. You've just heard that things are going wrong and that sales are down. You have a nasty feeling that they expect you to sort it out. Your heart is pounding and your mouth is dry. You're remembering when years ago there was an inexplicable sales collapse and it led to the closure of a division with lots of redundancies. Fortunately you survived. You remember the CEO's words: 'We've got a sales problem. What are we going to do to solve it?' You feel sick at the memory. Good mood? Right frame of mind? Don't be silly.

OK let's start somewhere else.

Don't panic

This is where experience kicks in. Research shows that nothing in life is quite as important as you think it is when you first start thinking about it. We all tend to worry about what could go wrong. Most humans, however optimistic, have gruesome imaginations: 'There's something wrong with the product. Complaints will flood in next. Then it'll be letters from solicitors. There'll be a product recall. I'll be blamed. They'll fire me without compensation. And walking back on the way home I'll be hit by a runaway lorry and lose the use of my legs. And my wife will leave me. And then I'll try to hang myself but the rope will break and I'll fall and break my arm... .'

But really, don't panic. You have a weapon at your disposal which can do almost anything. Your brain. First of all get things in perspective. As humans we are loss averse and the thought of losing sales we've regarded as ours by historic right is horrendous but we are also intensely pragmatic. We are good at fixing things. We are resourceful. We invented the wheel and harnessed fire. So what's a little sales decline?

What is the right frame of mind?

First of all you need to find a reasonable tone of voice… because people will listen to that.

Then as Wittgenstein told us 'don't think, look' by which I think he meant, use your eyes to see the stimuli and sources of inspiration that fuel thinking. Look, listen, wonder, challenge and read, most of all read, we all do far too little of that. Reading feeds the brain.

Next talk to those around in that reasonable tone of voice and listen to what they say.

 **tip**

> Listen to other people. We all need to bounce off others' ideas – and when we do that, thinking is almost physical in intensity.

Arjo Gosht, ex CEO and founder of the successful Brighton digital business, Spanner Works, which he sold to iCrossing[3] says he gets his ideas and really thinks when reading, at conferences and when travelling, but very rarely at meetings or sitting in an office. I think it depends on the office. Sitting in a book-lined room (never behind a partner desk – ghastly things – and increasingly not near a phone) can be fine… just be comfortable, relaxed and happy.

Next you need to use all your senses. It's well known that a smell can evoke a myriad of memories as can a piece of music. All psychological research proves that people who feel good think more clearly. You could try smiling more because when you do you'll think more clearly.

When we think about how suggestible our minds are we should consider the Florida Effect, and the Washington Experiment.

In the first, matched samples of respondents in America (let's call them A and B) were shown a list of words. In one list (Group A) the words 'Florida, sunshine, rocking chair, retired' appeared in the midst of a series of neutral words. In the other (Group B) these words were omitted. Researchers then compared the actual speed of walking and the posture of the respondents compared with what it had been before the test and with each other. Group B walked and had postures the same before and after. Group A, however, walked significantly slower and they were noticeably stooped afterwards. What was going on? Well Florida and the other words made respondents think of old people so they themselves mirrored this and started to act a little bit old themselves.

In the second experiment, which was done some time ago, when Deming[4] and his time and motion work was still very much in vogue, it was discovered that when basic ergonomic changes were made, like for instance repainting a room a new colour, then this change alone provoked an increase in productivity. However, productivity reverted to where it had been before shortly afterwards. This meant a lot of work for painters because whenever there was a change in paint colour the same thing happened. This was called the Washington Experiment.

So even if we aren't feeling wonderful we should be able to consciously suggest to our unconscious that all is reasonably well and that we are 'masters of our fate and captains of our souls' as poet William Ernest Henley put it. Just tell yourself that you are in charge and that all will be well.

You need to be a great question-master

As a rule you should take nothing for granted. Of all the environments we encounter the workplace and institutions of all kinds are infected with the 'because it's like that' syndrome. Even when rather hopefully we say 'let's start with a clean sheet of paper' no one does because no one can. We bring a lot of baggage and biases to any problem we face, many of these brought unconsciously. It's as though any meeting you have is full of a shadow group of prejudiced smugglers of recycled opinion.

So ask 'why?' a lot. Don't be palmed off with 'because I say so...' responses.

 **tip**

Always ask questions until you understand. Don't take the first explanation as enough if you don't get it.

Behave like an eight-year-old. If, for instance, a pricing structure is too complex for an eight-year-old to understand, it's probably too complex; period. This is something utility companies have belatedly discovered.

The rigorously repetitive 'why?' process was formalised by Toyota in its 'Five Why's' as it argued that the constant repetition of 'why?' eventually breaks down mendacity and uncovers the fib. (Jeremy Paxman has become famous by asking a recalcitrant, then Home Secretary, Michael Howard the same question 12 times. The interview is remembered as one of the toughest political interviews ever conducted. Mr Howard wriggled but did not, would not or could not answer the question.)

Interestingly, Jeremy Paxman was thoroughly courteous, even pleasant, throughout this session. It was the thoughtfulness and puzzled persistence that was so devastating. So interrogate carefully and look as though you are interested in and open minded about the answers as you try to expose strengths and weaknesses in others' arguments. The issue here is to have not made up your mind – you are investigating not judging. We are prone to prejudge issues or to try to see how a given problem resembles one we may have solved in the past. Don't do it.

Hone your memory – it's a great asset

Joshua Foer is a journalist and writer (*Moonwalking with Einstein: the art and science of remembering everything* is the book he wrote). He became interested in memory and especially the extraordinary feats of memory some achieve in remembering hundreds of numbers in sequence or the cards in several packs of cards. Intrigued that the seemingly impossible could be memorised he wanted to know more so he visited the USA Memory Championship. There've been 16 such championships in New York City. His interest deepened. So much so that in 2006, just out of interest, he trained for and entered the championship.

There he discovered people specialising in things like remembering as many decks of playing cards as possible, historic dates (events and historic years) and memorising the order of one shuffled deck of 52 playing cards as fast as possible. The world record for this is 21.90 seconds. There are 10 exercises in all.

Joshua was blown away. He realised he was in the presence of mental gymnasts of an extraordinary order. Yet in 2006 he entered just for interest and won it! Joshua Foer became US Memory Champion almost by chance. How? Well he explains on TED how you have to make those things you want to remember meaningful and tangible. He explains how techniques invented 2500 years ago still work today.

The lyric poet Simonides had a wonderful memory. During the excavation of the rubble of one Scopas' dining hall that had collapsed in an earthquake, Simonides (who'd luckily left before the disaster) was asked to identify each guest killed. Although their bodies had been crushed beyond recognition he successfully finished the task by remembering who was whom from their positions at the table before his departure. He later developed what became known as the 'memory palace', a system for mnemonics widely used until the Renaissance ...when things we needed to remember were printed so our memories weren't called on with quite the previous urgency.

Today of course our memory is on our iPad or smartphone. Today children at school are not taught to memorise. Today we've forgotten about memory. Yet memory today is still a vital thinking tool.

 **tip**

Since it's virtually impossible to be a great thinker without a reasonable memory, train your memory. Learn things by heart.

Imagine a lawyer who can't cross reference relevant cases. Imagine a toymaker who can't recall toys from the past similar to his latest idea. Imagine a writer who couldn't remember the references that enrich his assertions.

You cannot busk when you have poor memory. And in business you occasionally need that memory friend to remind you of a piece of evidence or of something that needs doing.

One of our biggest problems is our mind attic is stacked full of rubbish that we don't need. So, in specific areas we really want to focus on, we need to do a 'spring clean'. Learn some stuff by heart, put some structure around a subject in which you have a keen interest and see what happens.

Look after one of your precious assets. Having a good memory makes you so much more efficient, impressive and productive. But beware of one thing: our brains are brilliant at rewriting history and at editing our memories. What you remember may not be exactly how it happened especially when you were involved. You see there's a film editor in our brain editing history so we look better. It's not that difficult to train your brain to be better at remembering. But have the wit and instinct to ask the right question...was it all quite like we remember? Was Fred Goodwin quite that bad? I imagine that his own recollections of the RBS story would be very different to say Iain Martin's.[5]

Notes

1　Maria Konnikova is a Russian-American writer and journalist, living in New York City. She writes mainly about psychology and literature. *Mastermind* explores how to think, deduce, observe remember and imagine like Sherlock Holmes. It's very readable.

2　William James (1842–1910). American philosopher, psychologist and physician. One of the leading thinkers of the late 19th century he's been called the 'Father of American psychology'. He is much quoted and the author of many quotable quotes.

3　iCrossing operates as a global digital marketing agency. It's owned by the Hearst Corporation. Sales are estimated at around $200 million (with search representing 60 per cent of that). Headcount is around 1000.

4　William Edwards Deming (1900 –93) was an American statistician, professor, author and consultant. He worked in Japan, from 1950 onwards. He taught top business managers how to improve design, product quality, testing, and global selling by the application of statistical methods. He was believed to have been the true architect of Japanese industrial resurgence in the 60s and 70s.

5　Iain Martin is a political commentator, and a former editor of The *Scotsman* and former deputy editor of The *Sunday Telegraph*. He is the author of *Making It Happen: Fred Goodwin, RBS and the men who blew up the British economy*. The book somewhat racily describes the circumstances of the 2008 collapse of RBS. It left me wondering if this was the whole story. It has the immortal line in it: 'The assumption was that the "new thinking" made the world safer because it had originated from such clever people.' It's worth reading just for that.

CHAPTER 4

Read, mark, learn and listen (most of all listen)

Need to know more? It's time for R&L – research and learning

n problem solving you need that forensic interrogator on your side but you also need evidence that you need to consider. It's tempting to take a Malcolm Gladwell 'Blink' and on the flimsiest of data take a bit of a punt.

Philip Tetlock[1] was not being cynical when he suggested a pretty good reason for making sure our thinking was solid and underpinned by decent evidence. Hear the words of a wise man:

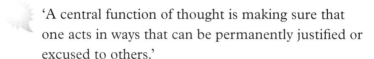

'A central function of thought is making sure that one acts in ways that can be permanently justified or excused to others.'

So do you know enough to understand? Have you got enough data, enough background information or enough facts – are there other things that need investigating? Can you quickly access the key issues in depth rather than having to start from square one and get busy reinventing the wheel?

The skill in quickly assembling evidence is as follows:

- **Reading** – anything and everything you can lay your hands on that might be relevant. Even if it's only marginally relevant, the effect it can have in fertilising your thinking can be magical. But, remember, don't believe everything you read. Keep asking questions. Internal reports and minutes can tell you a lot.

● **Using the web** – my source of wonder, frustration and rage. So much on the web is either wrong or awful. Focus on the wonder bit. It's the fact that you can lay your hands quickly on data and insights that help you frame a story. I worry that so many undergraduates have become better at 'cut-and-pasting' than writing essays nowadays but every wonder has its downside (like butter, sugar and alcohol).

● **Talking to people who know what's going on** – when General Electric embraced the concept of 'Work-Out'[2] in their business they recognised that getting people in the front line to think about how to solve the problems that they personally dealt with day by day was a self-evident breakthrough thought. Find the people close to the problem you are trying to solve to talk about it. Let them tell you what they see as the important elements. Listen and think about what they say.

● **Studying available data** – one of the most frustrating organisational problems is the destruction or archiving of the 'company memory'. As we change structures, downsize, relocate, merge and rationalise as all businesses do in the relentless quest to get more productive and competitive we mislay whole brain loads of knowledge. I was working on the Heinz account when I was in advertising and I persuaded a team to spend a fruitful Saturday to get together, read, fillet and summarise cupboards full of consumer research. It was, to borrow the term from taxi drivers, assembling 'The Knowledge'[3] in business. This knowledge is understanding how things work, what's been tried and how moving one moving part has an impact on other parts.

● **Getting first-hand experience** – in any situation try the product. And then try it again. Become a product addict.

Nothing ever beats first-hand experience. Lazy thinking is when someone says, 'I've tried Chateau Cheval Blanc 1989 I know what it tastes like.' Really? Really? In P.J. O'Rourke's enchanting 'The CEO of the Sofa' he and a friend do a wine tasting. Here's what he and his friend, Chris Buckley, said in an epic of wine tasting somewhere near the inebriated conclusion (mostly they'd been drinking inferior wines but there was this gem costing hundreds of pounds near the end):

'Wow is that complex? Is it the Big Boy?

'We'll have to drink several glasses to be sure.'

'P.F.G.'

'Is that a technical term?'

'Pretty f*****g good.'

'It's the Big Boy.'

'Definitely the Big Boy.'

You need to drink it to experience it adequately and freshly. And this applies to anything.

Plan better with good lists, priorities and editing

Brian Tracy, author and speaker, says: 'Every minute you spend in planning saves 10 minutes in execution.' He then converts this to a return on investment which seems overly elaborate but the point is a good one nonetheless – look at the map and think about where you want to go before you start the journey.

 **tip**

Lists of things to do are essential. Write down what you need to do.

Chef Anthony Bourdain says this:

'I'm a list fanatic. Write it down on a list and there's far less chance that you will ever find yourself beginning a sentence with the pathetic excuse 'sorry – I forgot to…'. The very process of writing a list clarifies and focuses the mind. Write enough of them and you will begin to think in lists, automatically prioritising.'

Even the most techie people I know keep a notebook (preferably a Moleskine) in their pockets so they can create a running list not just of things to do (especially the really urgent things) but so they can capture their thoughts in real time as they occur to them.

Ways to focus on critical thinking vary from doodling to think walking to dreaming or visualising to using a whiteboard to group thinking to creating hypothetical plans called 'strawmen' to using trial and error hypotheses. I find exercises using PowerPoint as a way of simply structuring an argument can be enormously helpful. This is all about planning which, done well, saves time and makes for better thinking, but remember John Lennon and stay alert: 'Life's what happens to you when you're busy making other plans.'

Daryll Scott, NLP expert and practitioner, puts this need for alertness neatly. He suggests that some fill their head so full of contingency plans for things that might happen that they are in theory prepared for everything. The trouble is 'everything' is likely to be a very big number. It's far better to plan well and then get yourself into a good, prepared mindset so you are 'prepared for anything'. Steve Peters is the writer of *Chimp Paradox* and psychological coach to the British Olympic Cycling Team. He's Australian, he's spare in his delivery and before him he carries an enormous reputation. At a briefing session with a bunch of wannabe Olympic performers he walked into a room full of awestruck anticipation and said:

'Good morning. There are just three things to remember:

1. *Life's unfair.*

2. *They keep moving the goalposts*

3. *You can only do your best.'*

Finally, editing.

The brain does this (the whole time). Literally between the ages of 12 and 20 when, as the brain grows, so a process of pruning unneeded neural pathways takes place. Pruning (as we know in nature) is good. Pruning your thoughts, getting rid of some of the straggly ones is a good thing. The essence of almost everything in life is that 'less is more' which is less a call for restraint than a call for a focus on quality. When Picasso was asked if sculpting a horse's head was really difficult he said it wasn't really that difficult. All he had had to do was chip away those bits that didn't look like horse. Simples!

The allies and the tools

Asking colleagues, peers, employees and thinkers 'what do you think?' is brilliant

Do not confuse consultation and listening to people with meetings. There are some who can't wait to get in a room and have a long meeting. But I believe meetings are the biggest enemy of thinking that there is, although one-to-one or small thinking groups (less than five) can achieve a lot.

Asking your colleagues 'what do you think?' is likely to provoke some action.

But there is a word of caution.

 **tip**

Sometimes asking people what they think when this is either something they don't do very often or when they are seriously under-briefed, so the question is falling on a confused brain, is not such a good idea.

Several years ago ad agency Draft/FCB Hamburg made two films showing focus groups. The research, conducted by the made-up company Stone & Stone Limited, explored the concepts of 'wheel' and 'fire' with a group of bolshie cavemen. These spoofs had a deadly serious point to make about group thinking and bias. Clearly the wheel was dangerous and could run away, possibly over your foot. Fire was the wrong colour. 'Red? Red reminds you of blood and blood reminds you of death. Green would be so much better. And being hot makes it dangerous… you could burn yourself. Now if it were cool… .' So there you are. You now have a square wheel and cool, green fire. Civilisation? Let it wait.

There's a serious point about people thinking together. In a group they can talk themselves into massive risk aversion and protection of the status quo. Secondly, when asked for their views they can get infected with an undue sense of self-importance. Anyone who's run a focus group will recognise that moment as a self-appointed sage emerges and persuades others to follow him in his opinions.

A worrying example of this is in *The Wisdom of Crowds* by James Surowiecki, when an group experiment was staged. The group, containing stooges, was briefed to decide which of three lines was the same length as another separately shown line. They thoughtfully and perversely reach an absurdly wrong conclusion and unwitting subjects tended to be persuaded to go along with the 'planted' stooges 'so as to not stand out'. Group think can easily lead to group idiocy. Crowds are not always wise.

But they can be when a diverse group with different skills are asked to work together in thinking through a solution about a difficult problem. Letting different expertise co-exist to co-ordinate evidence can be enormously useful. Experiments have included comparing the performance on a set of quiz questions of a diverse cross-section of society with a group of university professors. The diverse group of nurses, hairdressers, taxi drivers, management consultants and teachers won... of course they did.

But James Surowiecki had two examples which compellingly show that an average crowd will, on average, get a gauged judgement about right. One example was about 800 people judging the weight of an ox at a county show. Averaged out their guess was exactly, eerily, right to the nearest pound.

The second involved the loss of an American submarine in 1968. The US Scorpion disappeared on its way home after a tour of the North Atlantic. No one had any idea where it was. So a naval officer called John Craven created a series of scenarios for a diverse team of mathematicians, submarine specialists, salvage men and so on, and asked them to make their best guess of where the Scorpion was based on the very limited information they had. He aggregated their guesses using Bayes's law of probability. This measures a *degree of belief*; it then links the degree of belief in a proposition before and after accounting for evidence. The collective views interpreted using this theorem or law came up with a location very close to the actual location (although interestingly not particularly close to any one individual guess).

Generally the trouble with meetings is they include a large slug of didacticism plus a paranoid quest for 'alignment' and minutes that no one is very unhappy with nor, indeed, happy with either.

But the good thing about letting opinions flower and collide and shape other opinions is that one might just get a thoughtful and useful end result.

 **tip**

Meetings are usually meetings of egos. What we need are real meetings of minds.

Don't always trust experts

Research shows that we stop thinking for ourselves when an expert starts talking but as Warren Buffett tells us: 'You have to think for yourself.' Indeed not knowing very much about something can be a condition from which you have to work much harder to find out what that something is all about and are therefore forced to be more alert and think for yourself.

 **tip**

It's when you're learning that you think most lucidly.

An interesting example of experts getting it wrong was in a hospital in Cook County, Chicago, where a spike in post-operative infections broke out. After intensive research it was discovered it was caused by the doctors failing to wash their hands enough. These were experts who were very busy and who believed they were washing their hands but did a kind of mental shortcut and simply missed out a process in a routine. It's rather like an experienced driver failing to adhere to the speed limit and arguing until blue in the face that it was impossible he'd transgressed. The irony of this particular story is that at a meeting to discuss this issue, swabs taken from attending doctors showed their ongoing levels of hygiene still continued to be below standard.

Experts can be so clever they make assumptions that mere mortals like us don't understand. Nassim Taleb said of the tribe of bankers in the crash of 2008 that they had 'too much smoke, complicated tricks and methods in their brains so they started missing very elementary things'.

 **tip**

> Just because you don't understand something do not assume you are wrong.

Mr So-clever-it-hurts may have made a thinking error and simply exceeded the speed-thinking limit. Get people to take you through it again and again until you or they are clear.

What would your role models do?

Humans love a series of things like heroes and villains, results with winners and losers, playing together, my team versus your team. All this reduces thinking to a primary school playground level (psychologists have a ball with all this). Early on in life we begin to think that life is a zero sum game. And at school and in the workplace we begin to think it's more important to win than be smart. It's arguable that ethical teaching is very shaky and that cheating in a minor way is glossed over. Certainly small-scale cheating (we sometimes behave like fibbers but not liars, cheats but not felons) emerges as a norm in psychological tests when the chances of getting away with it seem pretty well non-existent.

People commonly use the language of the playground, and the incentives of reward and punishment which go with that. Bullying in the workplace is as prevalent as sexism. I heard my grandsons chanting 'boys are in, girls in the bin' so it starts at five. Then the girls started up 'no... girls are in, boys in the bin'. Ah. One all, I guess.

In work we all have role models like Jeff Bezos, Mark Zuckerberg, Richard Branson and the late Steve Jobs, all of whose greatness

comes with some complex personalities. All of them are creators, entrepreneurs, independently spirited and probably much
too disobedient to be just employees. Role models tend not
to be managers. Yet in our real world not our dream world of
being billionaires ourselves, we know people whom we admire
and aspire to resemble. Current management thinking is that
all of us need a mentor, someone who helps us strengthen
our strengths and mitigate our weaknesses. But we also need
a sponsor – someone who acts as a role model. Someone who
helps us 'think' our way through the political minefields of the
modern business world.

Then there are the real thinkers like Seth Godin, Nassim Taleb,
Michael Lewis and Malcolm Gladwell whose ideas move and
shake the world of business a little. Why? What do they bring that
earns them the real gold medals of thought?

Three things:

1   They are all contrarians who make us stop and reboot our
    brains.

2   They all speak basic, dirt-on-my-shoes English.

3   They all spend their lives looking for interesting ideas.

Think about these three qualities. You won't learn to be a real
thinker and problem solver without them.

 **tip**

> You need to be a bit of a rebel, be down to earth and have a real
> sense of curiosity.

Understand what data can do

'Big data' is transforming the way we think and analyse stuff. We
have discovered that correlation has become more important

than causality. That what happens is more important than why it happens.

We know the increase of information is accelerating. For instance all the information and data that currently exists will double in the next three years. With more information we need less exactness. Nowadays an equation $2 + 2 = 3.9$ is good enough. But sometimes $2 + 2 = 1$ (when one of the 2's is a box of oranges and the other 2 bottles of vodka and the 1 is a huge amount of screwdriver cocktail – QED). So don't even take maths for granted.

Today social media and CCTV may be more useful research tools than anything else we have. Google Translate has extraordinarily proved to be the best translation service around. The software uses 'corpus linguistics' techniques, where the program 'learns' from professionally translated documents, specifically UN and European Parliament proceedings but increasingly from all kinds of documentation – lots and lots of sources – big, big data. Intriguingly they say it improved when the linguists they'd hired when they started up (well you would want linguists in a translation service wouldn't you?) left the business because they wanted linguistic perfection, whereas this is a product of big data which is not that subtle.

The existence of robust data removing the tabloid use of anecdote allows us to spend more time using our brains to think rather than using them as pickaxes to mine for information. Anyone who tells you that guessing is more fun than knowing hasn't come across the thrill of irrefutable information. But while the big data boom is still happening we have sufficient glimpses of that future to see that we'll be doing less intellectual 'grunt work' in the future and more intellectual 'stunt work'.

Getting the recipe right

Imagine the brain as an Aga. Imagine the business problem or opportunity as the recipe. Imagine carefully assembling all the ingredients of that problem plus some diagnostic seasoning. Remember that preparation time is what makes all the difference. And then heat it slowly... stirring occasionally. Then go away and refresh your mind as it cooks. This sounds easier than it is.

 **tip**

Forcing yourself to stop and think about something else really helps fresh thinking.

But this isn't just a slam it in the pan and hope for the best. It's what Anthony Bourdain described as follows:

'It's all about transformation – about taking the ordinary and making it extraordinary.'

We also have to try hard because no one ever got anywhere without thinking hard. In all the studies that have been done, praise that's given for the hard work and for the effort made proves more motivating and productive than when people are praised for their raw talent. The latter tend to crumble a little when the going gets tough whilst the former soldier on thinking how to work it out.

The increasing popularity of cooking, especially with men, is because you get to eat what you think – which, when you think about it, is a delicious thought.

Ten brilliant observations to help you think

1   **The human mind is lazy and makes intuitive jumps or 'guesses'.** But once you understand this you can calm the whole process down and begin to be more in charge. Think longer, go straight to conclusions less.

2   **We all worry too much what others think.** We should spend less time trying to please and more time thinking about how to fix things.

3   **We tend to think overconfidently about things we know about.** Try to come to each problem with a fresh and an open mind. The reason all leaders tend to end less well than when they started their job is that when they think they know it all, they stop thinking.

4   **We often think lazily using what we already know to the exclusion of new evidence.** There's nothing worse for most people than to find their pet theory disproved. And we hate changing our minds. Prove the exception. Keep thinking 'is there a better way?'

5   **We are always looking for patterns or trying to find other problems like ours to help in a short-cut solution.** Short cuts are irreversible in the short run (especially when thinking about things like hair.) Professionals take it easy, getting the lie of the land and thinking about what's next.

6   **We want to retain the status quo.** Humans are resistant to giving up what they've got (hence the brilliant success of storage companies). Until we destroy what's no longer needed we'll never start thinking as positively as we should.

7   **When we get excited (hot) we think differently than when we are in a normal (cold) state of mind.** How do you feel? Are you emotional or calm right now? Modify the way you approach your thinking accordingly. Be self-aware.

8   **A random number can influence our judgement and make it 'fudgement'. We call this an anchoring error.** This is a crude test of our suggestibility. Numbers are the last thing you should be looking at when making a decision.

9   **'Iatrogenesis' is when doctors make things worse by over-treating. Thus in our world by overthinking and doing too**

much we create more problems. Think about the very least you can do to solve a problem. Saves money, saves time, saves stress.

10   **'No battle plan survives contact with the enemy'.** Thinking needs to be flexible.

Being able to change your mind is the mark of a good thinker. Being able to change your mind is key to survival in the 21st century.

 **recap**

The more we know about how our brain works, the better we'll be at using it to its utmost. Critical thinking becomes easier when we know the ten problems above are not insuperable and can, by training the brain, be fixed. Think about thinking. Yes, that will probably be unfamiliar advice but the more you work on how to be a better thinking machine the smoother will be your ride through work.

Notes

1   Philip E. Tetlock is the Leonore Annenberg University Professor of Psychology and Management at the University of Pennsylvania.

2   Work-Out was developed by GE with Schaffer consultants. Designed to demolish the inertia found in big organisations, people closest to the issues that need solving are brought together in intensive two-day thinking sessions. It's claimed that implementation of the best ideas is carried out over a maximum of just 100 days.

3   'The Knowledge' is what the Public Carriage Office, who regulate London cab drivers, call knowing how to get from anywhere to anywhere in London using the simplest, quickest route and which they test in exacting verbal examinations of prospective taxi drivers.

PART 4

Decision-making

Making a decision is a hard 'thinking' process. It actually creeps up on most of us when we aren't quite aware of it. Our unconscious intuition is hard at work whilst we imagine that we are being forensic and rational. So it's good to know what's going on because knowing can help us be better at managing the process and eliminating some of the human frailties that get in the way. Too much of our time is usually spent worrying if we'll *look* decisive rather than whether we are making the best decision, given all the circumstances and all the interests involved. In short, whilst we praise speed in business, decision-making is not a process to be undertaken lightly or fast. The good news is that being a thoughtful decision-maker is a skill we can learn. As the late Jim Greenwood rugby coach said, 'The real art of management is well-judged risk-taking.' The next few pages examine and give you tips on how to think your way to good judgement.

CHAPTER 5

Deconstructing the decision-making process

What happens when we make decisions?

Most of us think it's quite straightforward. We're asked 'what do we think?' so we sit down and look at the pros and cons of making decision A, B or C. We then, probably, consult a few colleagues. We assess the data. We may commission some original research. We consider a number of things about what the right decision is according to:

- the needs of the business;
- what our superiors and those who report to us will think;
- the probability of successful implementation;
- what we personally want and how each decision will make us look in the short and medium term and how it might affect our careers;
- what risks are involved that may not be immediately apparent.

But this means this: already it isn't a piece of simple, binomial work; we're way beyond tossing a coin here.

But it's actually much more complex than even this. There's a relatively new scientific field known as 'decision neuroscience'. Our thoughts, though a bit diaphanous and abstract, are shaped by specific neuronal circuits in our brains. Here is what Christian Jarrett[1] says in his book *30-Second Psychology*:

'*The new field is uncovering those circuits, thereby mapping thinking on a cellular level. Although still a young field, research in this area has exploded in the last decade, with findings suggesting it is possible to parse out the complexity of thinking into its individual components and decipher how they are integrated when we ponder.'*

 **tip**

Never underestimate making a decision. Think hard and make sure you've covered all the angles.

But rather than finding this quote especially helpful, I have been tortured by Barrett's and similar insights from Kahneman, Dennett, Taleb, Finkelstein and others into thinking something rather odd. And that is this: what had until now seemed part of the meat and drink of being a successful businessperson is in fact rocket science. Because it's so difficult, so very difficult, it should probably be restricted to a specialist group of experts called 'The Deciders'.

I want to tell you about an experience I had which demonstrates this issue outside the field of business but which is relevant to it.

Why I learnt to drive again

Having been driving for 40 odd years it was distressing to get my first and only summons for speeding. It was just after returning from holiday, when I'd been two things – relaxed and late – and I was driving like a prince and making up time. It was a camera that got me and as it flashed I thought… well you know what I thought.

I was offered the option of a fine and endorsement or attendance on a 'Speed Awareness Course' for a similar sum of money to the fine. At that point I made my first decision. I said 'yes' to the course. Ironically it was held at Brighton Race Course where presumably they are very aware of speed.

What was fascinating was the shift in my thinking that the course provoked, changing me from being an implicit thinker (someone who does what they do unconsciously) to an explicit thinker (back to being a learner driver and worrying about where your feet are). Over the course of two hours I underwent observation tests, reaction tests and was lectured at. I learned how putting your groceries on the back seat could mean the humiliation of being mugged fatally by a tin of baked beans if you braked suddenly or had a collision. How we failed to look far enough forward when we drive, for instance, to being able to anticipate a tractor coming from a hedge lined road in the far distance. And that white patch in the field on the left (hoar frost) which suggests what that shaded patch 100 yards ahead on the road might be… well? Sadly at the speed you've been driving you'd have just passed that patch were it not for the fact that it indicates black ice on the road, meaning that you've spun off into a ditch and, sorry, are dead.

My confidence (no, my overconfidence) was demolished and my mind rebooted. I became a non-stop decision machine who talked through his second-by-second decision-making to his wife when they next drove together: 'For heaven's sake shut up Richard, this is mad.'

Do all policemen drive like this the whole time I wondered? Is it a good system for making better decisions? Or isn't it just very annoying?

 **tip**

> Going through how and why you are making a decision step by step can be a very illuminating experience.

In fact in business we increasingly need to be at Advanced Drivers' level of competence when it comes to decision-making so there's not only a paper trail there's also a thinking trail which underpins the decisions we make. We need this because if called to account, saying 'I did it because it seemed like a good idea at the time' simply won't wash any more.

The most impressive part of the Speed Awareness Course was how it changed my behaviour. I now rigorously obey the speed limit – yes even the 20 mph regulation which covers most of Brighton – and I've refreshed my sense of risk. What most of all struck which me was how risk-blind I'd become, how unconscious of the context in which I operated. Quite simply I wasn't as ready for anything as I should have been. I was just taking things for granted because 99 per cent of the time I could.

Back to driving your business (rather than your car)

Create a 'decision-awareness course' so you can reboot your decision-making behaviour and most of all think about the following:

- your skills (and your limitations);
- the resources available to you (people, time and money);
- the constraints on your decision-making (politics, governance, stakeholders plus people, time and money);
- the culture and history of risk in the business.

Already the straitjacket of pragmatism has begun to tighten round you because making a decision is about a lot more than getting it right on paper. It's about making sure it 'plays well' across a broad bunch of people and it's about whether you can shepherd it through so it's accepted in theory and, eventually, it succeeds in practice.

You should start by asking the simplest of questions: 'What's this decision for?' First and foremost know what you want to achieve. Every decision that needs to be made will reach you with incomplete data, with differing views, with a series of choices to make. Ask why it needs to be made and what it seeks to solve and for whom. Peter Drucker warns us that a decision process 'starts not with facts but with opinions'. But whatever you do be wary of quick fixes... black and white thinking doesn't solve tough issues. The rule is WYSIATI – 'what you see is all there is'.

The changing business context

There are a series of factors that influence almost every decision we make:

- globalisation,
- technology,
- digital media,
- gender mix,
- generation Z.

Don't worry. I'm not trying to overcomplicate things, it's just not quite as simple as it used to be. And because it isn't we have to be mindful of a series of new perspectives.

Globalisation influences price structures and competition in a way that a decade or so back we simply hadn't foreseen. Technology changes the speed, accuracy and control we have. IT systems are so expensive, so frail and so liable to go past their sell by date we can't ignore the influence they have on corporate decisions, especially as human nature is so averse to giving up on things (look at IT systems in the NHS or BBC). Digital and social media mean no corporations can really have secrets any more. All decisions are transparent. And as regards gender issues: in a previously rather alpha male world more women are getting top jobs, and the more considered approach to risk that many women have influences the whole decision-making process. (I'll talk much more about women at work in the sections on empathy later on.) And finally, the new generations who tend to feel about life, the world and about business models a bit differently from older people.

Mix this lot together and the world of decision-making has changed a lot. Over 40 years ago on a management training course at what was then RHM Foods the facilitator threw an exercise at us:

'You believe the bakery producing your best-selling products may have been contaminating a local river. What do you do?'

It seems simple enough. Report it. Sort it. Take the hit.

Not in 1970... the group agonised over how to avoid being found out and carrying on as normal. Ethics took a back seat to capitalism. It was rather depressing. It occurred to me then, and I think this is now a constant truth, which we should bear in mind whenever we make decisions. Do not lie.

 **tip**

We are our own biggest competitor. Nothing the other guy does will ever damage us as much as we damage ourselves.

Note

1   Christian Jarrett is a British writer specialising in psychology and neuroscience. His next book is *Great Myths of the Brain*. A cognitive neuroscientist by training, he became a full-time writer after a spell of post-doctoral research at the University of Manchester.

CHAPTER 6

Become better at decision-making

How to make better decisions

fter all the qualifications I've just provided you probably feel like a trainee ice skater carrying a dozen eggs across the ice with the gruff command 'don't you dare break any'.

Don't worry, think of all these caveats and qualifications as background music to the hard-core decisions on which we need to focus in business.

brilliant tip

Identify the size of the prize and what it takes to win that prize.

What follows are a series of tips about getting yourselves in the best mindset to make better judged decisions and be seen as thoughtfully decisive not an impulsive gambler. Most of us would probably prefer to be seen as calm and logical, making well-argued decisions, whilst by now we all know that the reality of this is that logic is in the backseat trying to make itself heard. But we can tilt things in logic's favour.

Ten brilliant tips

1. Use your experience

'Successful decision-making is propelled by the kind of knowledge only built up through deep experience.' This is what Matthew Syed, former world champion table tennis player and now author and journalist, thinks. Patrick O'Sullivan, Chairman of Old Mutual, talks of the need to immerse yourself over time in a job so the logic of what you are learning becomes itself embedded in your sub-conscious. McKinsey in 1997 – pre-Enron – argued in its 'war for talent' theory, that domain specific skills and experience mattered much less than superior cognitive reasoning. Events have proved it wrong.

2. Apply confidence, leadership and learning

So, yes, experience is critical in providing the background against which better decisions are made. But there are four extra qualities we should seek in the successful decision-maker:

- self-confidence;
- leadership – the ability to take others with you;
- the desire to learn and an ability to learn from failure (by the way, beware the decision-maker who's never got it wrong);
- a preference for thinking rather than justification... it's not being right it's getting it right that matters.

3. Give yourself room to think

We all need the space and time in which to think. Previously, rather brutally perhaps, I've pointed out the tough scrutiny under which business people operate in today's world. But research demonstrably shows we think and we decide better when we don't have to explain all our decisions on a step-by-step basis. When work in progress is pulled apart it's unhelpful. Imagine being judged on what a half-cooked dish tasted like.

4. Embrace confusion and crises

The thinking process leading up to a decision can be rather messy. We should go through a state of puzzled confusion and we should discover new things because this will lead to better thinking. So too can a 'good crisis' which can force us to focus on key issues and concentrate the mind. Sometimes the stressful demands of having to make a decision can blind us to the real reason the decision has to be made. But usually when you're in trouble the reason will be self-evident.

5. Break a decision into pieces

When a problem or a scenario is complicated it's often helpful to break what needs to be decided upon into separate components. If a situation is too big to get your head around don't try to do so, ask yourself what the three or so key elements are so you can think each of them through individually. All the research done by psychologists shows complexity of choice and data overload can cause 'brain freeze' (that's the condition when you feel you couldn't even tie your shoelaces). In research, a simple test shows a box of chocolates containing a choice of six chocolates is much preferred to one with 30 choices. (Just remember 'fewer chocolate choices frees up the freezing brain'.)

6. Take a broad view

Often the clearest impact of a style of decision-making is seen in the slightly more black and white world of financial trading. Here's what David Blair, US Financial Consultant, says:

'Studies have helped us understand how we hold and trade stocks, and show how behavioural biases such as familiarity, overconfidence, narrow framing, trend chasing, the lottery effect, and home bias lead to poor decision-making.'

In broad framing, as opposed to narrow framing, you take a big picture view rather than looking for a quick gain or quick fix.

7. Look forward as decisions are about the future

Mindfulness proponents will recognise this piece of sound advice: only think about the future when making a decision. Do not worry or think about what went right or wrong in the past. What mindfulness helps us do is learn how to reflect. Deep reflection means not being disturbed; it means thinking in a way that absorbs us in the same way as when we read a deeply involving book, when time passes without our even noticing. Here's how psychologist Mihaly Csikszentmihalyi[1] put it:

'effortless concentration so deep we lose our sense of time, of ourselves and of our problem'.

8. Stop being stressed

Bad decisions get made through time pressure and chasing your tail. To help you, try thinking of issues and challenges as stories with plots and sub-plots not as dry, arid, 'business-y' things. The great thing about the language of stories is that they take us away from the world of jargon to the heart of things.

9. Train your gut and trust it

I've always believed in first training, then in trusting your gut. We know how important our intuition is, that it leads much of what we do. It's an uncomfortable thought that our intuition is in some sense a 'whatever, can't-be-arsed adolescent' when what we need is a responsible, mature magician, lightning reactor, memory man and expert at mental juggling. Stories of firefighters often figure in the studies of psychologists on decision-making. When asked, firefighters will tend to deny they make decisions saying, instead and modestly, that they just do what needs to be done. They think they don't make decisions because their instincts do the work. Such a judgement would also apply to footballers, or tennis players facing a serve of 150 mph which is faster than their thinking time and reaction time can cope with let alone make decisions about.

10. Use your experience; the more experience the better

Back to the beginning. Experience. It's the number of times we've encountered a situation which prepares us to make smart judgements. We must accept that we are not wholly rational beings, that we have prejudices and biases, that we are emotional and sometimes erratic. But we have something else. We learn. We like learning and we understand and improve as we do it. Making decisions is as much of a game, we learn, as is Matthew Syed's table tennis. Here's what he said again:

'Successful decision-making is propelled by the kind of knowledge only built up through deep experience.'

Visualise the consequences of your decision

Mindfulness tells us not to regret the past or be frightened of the future but to focus on getting the present right. Such advice manages to make most of us feel better when we are stressed but it doesn't always help us make better decisions.

Thoughtfulness, which is my version of what needs to follow mindfulness, is based on helping us do our jobs better. Its particular relevance to decision-making lies in its variance with mindfulness:

- We must learn from the past.
- We must manage the present.
- We must make decisions that shape the future.

Nearly all the executives I've spoken to anguish more about the possible reaction of people to the decision they have to make rather than the decision itself. They worry that someone who's given just rather grudging assent to a decision may cool in their support of it or even change from lukewarm pro to being in open disagreement of the 'I had the feeling it was wrong all along' kind.

Visualising the future and examining potential scenarios created by different decisions is the key to being a great leader. Think about how this decision will impact on you and others. What fall-out might there be? How can you think of managing this? Is there anything you've not thought about? Is there any party you've not covered off?

In the past, there was some control of the media and of communications in a business. It was a tap you could turn on and off. You couldn't stop it dripping but you hoped no one would notice. Today that drip, even in the off position, remains effectively a steady flow to the despair of authoritarian governments and managements throughout the world. This means all your thinking about fall-out has to be up front and why the most professional companies are brilliant at crisis management. The more deeply we think the better we prepare for the unexpected.

And now we have values too

The world has changed. Will McInnes runs Nixon McInnes. It's based in Brighton. The company is a digital transformation company specialising in people and culture. It believes passionately in CSR (corporate social responsibility) and it is angry. Aren't you, Will?

'People say business is broken. You know what? I agree. Screw how that kind of business is: the 20th century rapacious school of business that ruined its people, corrupted its environment and lumbered like an eyeless, earless giant from room to room, smashing plates, breaking doors down and filling its pockets with gold coins. We've had enough. We the workers, the shareholders, the managers, the community members, the entrepreneurs and the everyday folk.'

A lot of people feel like Will. Especially women and a lot of generation Z too. In other words, the people who'll be running our world in the next 20 years who have *real* values. They believe that business is not boring, conventional, MBA driven or only about profit. Bill Bernbach,[2] the most famous ad man ever, said:

'A principle isn't a principle until it costs you money.'

Bill would like the way things are today, and the need for cut-though, 'bringing the dead facts to life' as he put it, is what is so strongly needed. He'd most of all like what Gary Hamel,[3] the management guru, described as the need to 'reclaim the noble'. Here's his scenario to test any decision-maker's resolve. Imagine you run this hypothetical company:

- Your mum has her life's savings in your business.
- Your COO is your younger sister whom you adore.
- Your employees are your best friends dating back to childhood.
- Your children and all their friends are your main customers.
- You don't need the money.

Would your decisions be different in this kind of business? Would they?

Why it helps to think loose and improvise

We make the mistake of getting stuck in the same groove; some-times even the most creative of us. The words designed to make anyone scream are our corporate template, our tried and tested formula and our company strategy (usually because there isn't one).

 **tip**

To think and make well-informed, inspired decisions we have to get outside that proverbial box and consider our situation from a different perspective.

This is what Professor John Kay of the LSE calls 'obliquity'. He says obliquity (pursuing our goals indirectly) is necessary because we live in a world of uncertainty and complexity; the problems we encounter aren't always clear – and we often can't pinpoint what our real goals are. Things change and people (whose behaviour is so often hard to predict) change too. Direct approaches are often unimaginative whilst 'muddling through' can sometimes be a much more productive answer.

In games like *Sudoku* the world is certain and static and some people act as if their world is like that too. But business is not a game any more and treating it like one with straightforward rules will fail. Business needs decision-makers whose decisions are driven by an ability to duck and weave according to circumstances.

Stories of improvisation beating the corporate plan abound but there are two that Malcolm Gladwell tells that I enjoy. Big corporate Goliath being outwitted and outgunned by the guerrilla tactics of David armed with his sling, the 1000 BC equivalent of a Remington XP-100 currently rated the most accurate hand gun in the world. David knew the outcome was certain provided he stayed out of lumbering Goliath's reach but what's baffling is that Saul and the others saw this contest quite differently as a one-sided toe-to-toe duel because that's how you did things in those days. They were thinking in direct 'like-we've-always-done-it' terms rather than 'let's-win-using-what-it-takes-to-win' terms.

In business, stories of small, loose thinking winners include Nike winning as a Vietcong upstart founded in 1964 against Adidas founded in 1948. Nike is now twice the size of Adidas. Likewise, Facebook was dwarfed by Myspace in June 2006 when Myspace captured 80 per cent of social networking traffic and Facebook had 7.6 per cent. Now Facebook has 1.3 billion users and Myspace only around 1 million. In the mobile phone market we've seen four major players, two moving from hero to zero in a rapid space of time – Motorola, Nokia, Apple and now Samsung. Decisions in this rough and tumble game are about life and death. The ball has been dropped in most markets and no one knows where it is. Better to improvise rather than pretend the ball's still in sight.

We all tend to overestimate power whether it's physical like Goliath's or exploited by people who feel they're expected to flaunt it. That's a high-risk strategy on their part but some seem to think it worth taking. Chuck Prince, ex-CEO and Chairman of Citigroup, certainly seemed to think so as he stated the defining quote on the very eve of the credit crunch:

'When the music stops, in terms of liquidity, things will be complicated. But as long as the music is playing, you've got to get up and dance. We're still dancing.'

You make decisions that solve problems by taking each on its merits and not being hamstrung by a rigid plan. Strategic planning in that old, slow, spreadsheet way can make one option blind. Remember what Mike Tyson said:

'Everyone has a plan till they get punched in the mouth.'

Why delaying decision-time is often good

It's strange, but we're reluctant to give up on what we've got. When businesses go wrong we behave like people on the *Titanic* refusing to believe that the worst can happen. Yet we have this insane desire to make decisions very fast. The two are in complete contradiction.

Almost all plans are beset by overoptimism on cost and timing. Consistently our sense of time is shaky – we never expect anything to go wrong and be late – we have a timetable in mind and we are incapable of accepting it's a work of hope and probable fiction. We are even worse with money. Pity the poor Scots who in 1997 thought their new parliament building, designed by Enric Miralles, was going to cost £40 million but when it was finished in 2003 the final bill was £431 million. I sympathised about this to a Scottish friend who said, 'Well it's not really like that – you see Westminster paid for it.'

Humans like making their decisions decisively and making them fast, showing courage, leadership and prescience, but once they've made a decision they are usually strangely intransigent about changing their minds (regardless of the circumstances). Mentally we have (as it were) no reverse gear. If nothing else should be clear, this state of mind is a very strong reason for taking it step by step and slowly, and for changing Conan the Destroyer to Conan the Cautious Tortoise.

✷ brilliant tip

To think decisively, open up debate with friends and colleagues and sometimes accept that not making a decision may be a good strategy.

Warren Buffett, whom I unashamedly quote from frequently, mainly because he's so smart, says, 'If I get an idea next week I'll do something. If not I won't do a damned thing.'

Slow down and think. The decision will be right when you make it then. And the opposition still won't know where the ball is.

But understand the odds in the gamble because all decisions are gambles

All decision-makers are taking a risk. But the biggest risk comes when you don't know what you're doing. Ignorance, like being lost, may sometimes be exciting but it's crazy to make a decision if you could shorten the odds in your favour by thinking longer and working harder. But even when you are as well prepared and with the best advisors you could have, any decision is still, by definition, a gamble. Understanding that may help you view decision-making more circumspectly.

Not that you'd think that any of this was true if you talked to most start-up businesses. Now to be fair we shouldn't expect them to be pessimistic. That's not in an entrepreneur's make-up, but the following figures are illuminating. Let's start with a fact. Only 35 per cent of start-ups survive more than five years, but in research by Daniel Kahneman:

- 60 per cent believe that they will survive longer;
- 80 per cent believe they have a better than a 7 in 10 chance of going for longer than five years;
- 33 per cent believe they have a zero chance of failure. (This one's extraordinary. I regard nothing as having a zero chance.)

Based on work by Richard Wiseman the optimists in the sample, by virtue of their mindsets, will quite understandably be shortening the odds in favour of surviving but even so this flight in the face of reality is a little surprising.

 tip

The lesson we need to learn is that some you win and some you lose. That's what the true entrepreneur thinks.

True entrepreneurs learn from failure and abort businesses which early on show no signs of going anywhere. The successful entrepreneur is not usually a romantic. They are hard hearted. Unlike most people they do not try to hang on to what they've got if what they've got doesn't seem worth hanging on to. Harvey Herman is an American. Like so many Americans I know he is wealthy, charming, a wonderful neomaniac (a lover and addict of that new-new thing). Every time I met him over the years he'd tell me about the latest wonder idea he'd had. The next year I'd see him and ask, 'How are the electronic sugar tongs going?' and he'd say, 'What a terrible idea that was. Sold it to Tate and Lyle for a good profit but I must tell you about my new concept', and he'd look at you and continue 'the dog treadmill or Lazer Weeder for faster gardening' and he'd have dropped or sold off each one before we next met, but always making a profit from the sales and never blushing that he'd made a mistake. He belonged to the school that the more decisions you made the more winners you'd have.

In a famous psychological experiment – 'the Iowa card experiment' – expert gamblers were asked to select cards from four stacked piles, two of which were marginally in their favour and two of which were marginally against them. Unconsciously they recognised those piles of cards that were stacked against them and acted accordingly – and this is the surprising point – *prior to consciously knowing* why *they were acting that way*. What I enjoy about this is it rather turns on its head the 'attitude determines behaviour' theory. It's also evidence that the lessons from deep experience stored in our unconscious memory are a key factor.

> Humans have this tendency to overdramatise and give too much weight to rare probabilities because we like vivid stories.

We look for headlines relating to incurable bird flu sweeping across Northern Europe, shark attacks off Fowey in Cornwall killing 20, a Eurostar train crashing into a herd of Charolais cows 30 minutes south of Calais, how a cluster of tarantulas are found in the bananas in a supermarket by a student and so on. Mention any of these and the average human will believe that the possibility that any of these events might actually happen is much higher than actuarial data would show. A lot of statistics are quite prosaic. The chances of dying from diabetes rather than an accident are four times greater.

Cordelia Fine[4] has identified a group who are much better forecasters and gamblers than the average:

'There's a category of people who get unusually close to the truth about themselves and the world. Their self-perceptions are more balanced, they assign responsibility for success and failure more even-handedly and other predictions for the future are more realistic. These people are living testimony to the dangers of self-knowledge. They are the clinically depressed.'

Michael Lewis,[5] in his book *The Big Short*, has a similar insight. He describes several of the key players in the creation of the credit default swap market who bet against the collateralised debt obligation (CDO) bubble and thus ended up profiting from the financial crisis of 2007–10. The book highlights the eccentrically antisocial nature of the type of person who bets against the market or goes against the grain. One (or more) of them suffered from Asperger's syndrome and refused to follow the herd.

The art of forecasting

We are bad at predicting because prediction is quite simply not a human skill. Film maker Sam Goldwyn ironically observed that it was difficult to predict, especially when it came to the future. Yet we'd like to think we are good at it. Successful businesspeople are lauded for their prescience but increasingly socio-economists are ruefully concluding that most forecasters are more reliant on luck than judgement. It's actually worse than that. Monkeys could probably do better over time than most bond traders. This is not to decry the fact that bond traders do try really hard, just that even those with reputations for infallibility, like Anthony Bolton, can falter. His Fidelity Special Situations fund grew an annualised 19.5 per cent over 28 years (that's astonishing; his reputation is well earned and he had an amazing Midas touch). But then he went to Hong Kong to manage the newly formed Fidelity China Special Situations PLC. This lost 34 per cent of its value in 2010–11. No one could have forecast this except those who believe regression to the mean is the norm in life.

Nassim Taleb has a friend called Fat Tony who made a lot of money shorting oil in the first Iraqi War. As squads of quantitative mathematical geniuses were doing spreadsheets factoring in everything from the history of Kuwait to the fuel consumption of the new Ford Focus he reflected that the market had already taken the key issues into account. In other words, the probability of war post the invasion of Kuwait by Iraq had been factored into the price of oil so when it happened the price would not rise as most forecast. Instead it would stabilise and then fall. He was right.

Our forecasting is usually driven by what happened in the past and our yearning for patterns and trends.

We are much better at seeing change than noticing when things don't change. Forecasters want tidy solutions and predictability. The curse of all forecasts is the 'idle percent'. When doing a sales' forecast, for instance, the request for a 10 per cent increase given a growing sector and increased marketing spend seems hard to resist. Ten per cent sounds easier than, say, a million more customers or existing consumers consuming another 20 pints or 30 platefuls each. We love trends but we seldom trend-spot really big changes in behaviour like the declines in smoking; and more interestingly perhaps, that there'd be supine acceptance of smoking legislation throughout the UK. The decline in alcohol consumption currently seems a surprise to many because the signs and noise of drunkenness on a Friday night are so vivid an experience. Personal experience overwhelms data for many.

We live in a business environment in which it is commonplace to make bold forecasts which are supported by a rather timid plan. Most of us dream of growth and better futures but are unprepared to change things to achieve them. We find it really hard to pare down the things we'll concentrate on, to focus and to decide which horse to back. We are cautious creatures because uncertainty (and danger) comes with adventure and venturing outside our comfort zone into the unknown. John Kearon, CEO of Brain Juicer,[6] has produced the best derogatory line I've yet come across on most research and the value it brings to decision-making and forecasting:

'heavy on numbers, light on insight, dead on arrival'.

There's a Yiddish proverb which rather splendidly captures the commonsense approach to planning and forecasting (but for it to be authentic in its delivery you must shrug as you say it): 'Provide for the worst; the best can take care of itself.' The trouble is, of course, as Cordelia Fine observed, our brains are reluctant to give processing time to nasty predictions so we tend to do things the other way round instead and assume all goes well; so in fact we provide extremely well for the best.

Looking into the future, not so much to get it right as to stimulate your understanding of the need to prepare for change, can be helped by trying this:

Write a spoof newspaper article or Wikipedia entry about your business 10 years from now. This will force you to make some decisions as to how the plot might resolve itself and what the key issues might be. Best assume you are a spectator and not a participant as this way your predictions will be more adventurous.

Notes

1   Mihaly Csikszentmihalyi is a Hungarian psychology professor, who emigrated to the United States at the age of 22. Now at Claremont Graduate University, he is the former head of the department of psychology at the University of Chicago. His major work is on creativity and happiness. His best known book is *Flow: The Psychology of Optimal Experience*.

2   Bill Bernbach (1911–82) was an American advertising creative director. He was one of the three founders in 1949 of the international advertising agency Doyle Dane Bernbach (DDB). He directed many of the firm's breakthrough ad campaigns (Avis, Polaroid, VW) and had a lasting impact on the creative team structures now commonly used by ad agencies today. He was also a genius, a seer and the father of advertising in the 1970s. He is why I hate *Mad Men* – they are so bad. Bill would have killed them.

3   Gary Hamel has been on the faculty of the London Business School for 30 years. He's an American management expert and founder of Strategos, an international management consulting firm based in Chicago. His most recent book is *What Matters Now*. He's highly regarded as a strategist and speaker.

4   Cordelia Fine is a Canadian-born British academic, psychologist and writer. Her first book, *A Mind of Its Own*, synthesises a large amount of cognitive research to show how the mind often gives a distorted picture of reality. She writes especially well

and enthusiastically about the 'vain brain' – the brain acting as motivator to write this book.

5   Michael Lewis, ex-investment banker at Salomon Brothers, is an American non-fiction author and financial journalist. His consistently brilliant books include *Liar's Poker*, *The New, New Thing*, *Moneyball*, *The Big Short: Inside the Doomsday Machine* and *Boomerang*. His book *Flash Boys*, about the high-frequency trading sector of Wall Street, was released in 2014.

6   John Kearon is a Unilever trained marketer who first went into advertising with Publicis, then formed his own innovation businesses and in 1999 Brain Juicer, a company designed to reinvent market research. It was voted the most innovative Research Agency in 2011.

CHAPTER 7

Heffalump-traps, sleeping-policemen and other pitfalls

There are a series of things you really mustn't do when making a decision. Here are the most obvious no-no's.

Ten brilliant tips on avoidance

1. Avoid thinking like an ass

I love the story of Buridan's Ass.[1] Dying in the desert, this ass realised he was equidistant from food and water. He was desperately hungry and he was desperately thirsty. But unable to decide which way to go to satisfy his needs he lay there in a quandary and died, dehydrated and starved. If you know that you have to make a decision and it's a 50:50 choice about what to do, think hard, assess both options and then make a decision. In this case the right answer was 'water'. Do not be an ass.

2. Avoid making up your mind prematurely

The single most common cause of bad decisions is using 'misleading prejudgements' and deciding what to do before hearing all or any of the evidence. It's quite hard to resist as our immediate instincts are at work chipping away at the problem before we are even aware of it. But we are also often 'square-pegs-into-round-hole-bashers'. Put that hammer away. Listen to what the whole story is.

3. Avoid inappropriate prevarication

'Stop and think' is the advice I've strongly given elsewhere but as always there are exceptions. When you can, take your time in making a decision. Do not rush when waiting longer might allow new light to be shone on a problem. But in a crisis or, to put it crudely, you're standing in the middle of a motorway with traffic hurtling towards you, reflection, thought and analysis are (or should be) the last things on your minds. When you are in a tight corner and the adrenalin is surging, rely on your instincts, trust your gut and get a move on.

4. Avoid being that man in the ivory tower

When I was a young account director in advertising, I was working on a French brand and after a very long and expensive photographic shoot I was told the CEO had asked to see the shots. He saw them. Word came back: 'Il a dit que… non.' Do not decide remotely like this if you want good results from those around you.

5. Avoid the dying dictator

The dictator is unwell but is also unused to other people having a point of view. There's a story about the Duke of Wellington, not the current one but the one who led the British Army at the Battle of Waterloo in 1815. Having been a great and a successful general, 13 years later he became Prime Minister. Patterns of behaviour are often ingrained. Asked by a friend after his first cabinet meeting how it had gone he said: 'Extraordinary thing but I gave them their orders and they wanted to sit around and discuss them.'

The day of the autocrat (with a very few exceptions is over). We live in collaborative times now where give and take and attentive listening marks the leader. Oddly politicians still call consultation and listening 'weak leadership'. As the Duke of Wellington might have said: 'Deuced odd thing that.'

6. Avoid being hungry

Making decisions on an empty stomach can lead to erratic decision-making. Kahneman did some work in Israel as a young man and discovered a phenomenon amongst Israel Parole Court judges whose propensity to allow parole before lunch was widely different and less generous than after they'd eaten. Do not make a big decision on an empty stomach.

7. Avoid small numbers

They call the use of anecdote and small samples 'the law of small numbers' and it's a very bad practice. How often in the middle of a seriously argued case will you hear someone, who's otherwise very sensible, say 'well that's all very well but in my experience…' which, when probed, means 'I observed on one occasion' which, flying in the face of quantified data may not be treated seriously, but nonetheless changes the trajectory of discussion.

8. Avoid being smug about success

Success can confuse thinking and decision-making. We remember when we made a great call, a judgement that really paid off. We always (being human) want to repeat that. The major issue I have with some non-executive directors is when they use the 'when I decided right' argument. Much stronger would be the 'when I made a disastrous decision'. Then we'd all listen: but you don't hear that very often. My favourite example of the confusing effect of success is in Mel Brooks' *The Producers* in which the sure-fire box office disaster on which the producers have based their gamble turns out instead to be a huge hit provoking the horrified response from Max Bialystock and Leo Bloom: 'What did we do right?'

9. Avoid reducing your chances

Making decisions when you are very tired, jet lagged, drunk or are working in a foreign language (that probably includes

American by the way) is best avoided. Strangely some psychologists, including Maria Konnikova, suggest that we are better at solving insight problems when tired or drunk because our executive function is inhibited. But in making decisions? No, never.

10. Avoid shortcuts, sleeping on the job and short changing

The brain has a brilliant way of taking the easy way out. Here are a few things to avoid.

When thinking about a difficult decision we'll often:

- Ask ourselves an easier question (in other words unconsciously just change the brief to something we know we can do better as opposed to struggle with something that seems intractable).

- Or move on to something we like doing more as opposed to this difficult thing which is the problem we have. Maintaining our attention is hard especially when facing the need to decide.

- Or go into mental hibernation. 'I'll sleep on it' is a good idea when we are thinking and, as we know, it works. The Aga of our mind gets cooking. Yet the urge to hide from making a decision, going into denial, is common and, because it's rather cowardly, it's something the hibernator denies.

- Or simply fail to look hard enough. Magicians rely on our faulty eyesight. We see pretty clearly dead in front of us – things that are in the spotlight – but there's darkness on the periphery of our vision. We know we have a deep-rooted laziness. Apart from misleading prejudgement, a failure to do all the homework and really scrutinise the evidence is one of the biggest reasons for poor decision-making.

Decisions are driven by our emotions and responded to emotionally

We know how important our emotions are and that our instincts are the powerful engine of our thinking. We think we are coldly rational whilst it's our intuition that's in charge. This makes for a more interesting but less predictable life. Decisions are reached by us working hard at trying to get emotions and logic aligned, trying to get our opinions and our analytical thinking side working as a team. But here's what's really going on:

> Benjamin Libet[2] earned fame for his work using MRI scans to help interpret what happens during the decision-making process. He concluded that our sub-conscious is making the decision that is fed to our conscious and that there's a time lag of half a second between the two. Whilst interesting I'm not sure what we are to do with this except to suggest that when this happens, when in other words the decision we are seeking arrives in our mind, we'd do well to think 'good, that's helpful, now let's question again whether this is the right or the only decision'. In other words, rigorously question yourself.

A key to good thinking is always going to be to strengthen your resistance to taking even your own feelings for granted. Trust your gut (but only up to a point). Always say, 'Hang on… can I find a better solution… is this necessarily the best and only decision?'

When we've decided, having flexed our thinking, that it probably is the best decision and we take it, we then still have to carry others with us. Marketing our decisions is the really hard bit, harder than making the decision itself.

 **tip**

Work on your sales script to ensure emotional as well as rational buy-in is achieved.

 **tip**

Then focus on tightening the debate, reducing the amount of wriggle room anyone in a team has to recant on endorsing the decision they've agreed.

This isn't being authoritarian, it's just being realistic. A decision isn't going to be a real decision until it gets buy-in.

Presentation matters too. If a surgeon tells you either that a given procedure gives you a 10 per cent chance of dying or that it gives you a 90 per cent chance of surviving (and rationally you know that these are the same thing) the chances are you'll see the latter option as much superior. And that happens in research with comparative approval scores being respectively 50 per cent and 84 per cent.

Indeed I'd guess 90 per cent of decision-making is an exercise in selling the decision and making it happen for most people. Cognosis,[3] the management consultancy, has research that strongly shows three key results:

- Most strategies need to be pitched emotionally at the people who have to make them work if these strategies are to succeed…
- but most strategies fail in execution…
- because few strategies are bought into with any enthusiasm by middle management and below. Indeed the further one

gets from the C-suite the more sceptical the reception is likely to be.

Not everyone thinks making decisions is that hard. Here's what George Bush said:

'I don't spend a lot of time taking polls around the world to tell me what I think is the right way to act. I've just got to know how I feel.'

I hope, if nothing else, that remark underlines just how important rigorous thinking really is when making decisions.

Making the results of decisions happen

When Apple was voted the number two logistics operation in the States, Steve Jobs would have been incredibly proud that his innovation rated business was also cutting it in execution. Because in the end, execution is what really counts if you're a customer. Looking good on the page or the advertisement but falling short on the plate, the road, the desk or when you wear it, is worse than disappointing. So making the decision work in reality is the real challenge. Why spend hours agonising over strategy, days stumbling towards a hard fought for and hard thought through decision for the performance to turn out to be a lemon?

 **tip**

We'll be judged by what we delivered, not by what we decided to deliver.

A champion of execution is Amazon which delivers on a Monday morning what you ordered from them on a Sunday afternoon. They execute by satisfying what we suddenly decide we wish to have regardless of what were previously unassailable frontiers (like night and time). Leon Kreitzman[4] predicted this breakthrough in his book *The 24 Hour Society* 15 years ago, but even he might not have foreseen quite how life-changing it can be to be able to remedy a memory deficiency over a birthday using the masters of execution, Amazon.

This means the bar the rest of us have to match now is really quite high. It's completely unacceptable to say, 'It will be with you by the end of the week.' If Amazon can do it, so can you. This means that in making decisions you have to consider if you have the will, the energy and the resource to deliver what you decide you want to deliver in the way that people have come to expect.

Visit a Next and then visit an M&S store and you may begin to understand the tightness of focus and delivery of expectation of the former is not quite matched by the more *laissez-faire* latter. You begin to understand why, relatively speaking, Next is doing so well.

People whose decisions and follow through are consistently aligned are companies like Diageo, BMW, Ikea, Starbucks, McDonalds and B&Q. But aren't these rather large stores with lots of training procedures? Isn't it true, as E. F. Schumacher[5] said, that 'small is beautiful'? Isn't the trouble with big companies that they tend to be slow, lumbering and lacking in innovative ideas?

But the trouble with small companies is (in my experience) that the independence of spirit sometimes seeps into the way they treat their customers. Imagine a wet Saturday in Hove at 5.30 pm. The need for coffee is strong. Yet the trendy, characterful, doors-wide-open-to-the-elements independents are closing or have closed. Costa Coffee remains brightly warmly and welcomingly open. It's not about ownership, it's about just one decision.

 **tip**

The key decision to make is this: what will our customers want?

Gary Hamel says that people want to do the right thing. He then adds, but they need help with understanding what right is. The right thing is always to perfect customer service, to turn it into an art not just a process. But it cannot be perfected unless a decision-maker in a big or small company can visualise in detail the impact each decision made actually has all through the business, out to the end user.

Examples of bad decisions we can learn from

In their book *Think Again*, Finkelstein, Whitehead and Campbell[6] ask how risk can be reduced and deconstruct some famously bad decisions. Or were they? Nearly all seemed a good idea at the time but proved disastrous because something was missed or ignored or occasionally because no one said, 'Whoa!' Sam Goldwyn, who was a cantankerous old dictator, had a wicked wit. But when he said this he probably meant it:

'I don't want to be surrounded by yes-men; say what you think even if costs you your job.'

Here are a few such examples.

 disasters

When Quaker bought Snapple

Read *Think Again* for the full story. Quaker had bought Gatorade in 1983 and made a spectacular success of it. It then bought Snapple thinking that it could repeat the trick. After all it was just another fizzy drink company. The trouble was Snapple was a cult drink with little going for it except a Jabberwocky of a name and Leonard Cohen attitude to life. Of all the brands least likely to be integrated or imprisoned by a corporation like Quaker, Snapple was it. In early 1994 I pitched for their advertising. I know an Al-Qaeda brand when I see it and these boys, who were clearly in the latter stages of priming the business for sale, wanted to put their 'rebel yell' of a brand into suit and tie to maximise the price. If only Quaker had asked me. Pity because Quaker suffered a death blow and Snapple lost most of its shine. Don't mix oil brands with water brands – it doesn't work. And never muck with cults. Quaker might as well have tried to take over and market Leonard Cohen.

Lesson: This was an avoidable bad decision involving a misreading of culture and its importance provoked by the Quaker Chairman's prejudgement about the successful formula based on his Gatorade triumph.

When Heinz decided to mess with its ketchup

Over 15 years ago I was working as a consultant with Heinz UK on a number of issues but biggest of these was on the 'Real Food Initiative', a top to bottom clean-up of the image and reality of the Heinz food ingredient purity story. The story was impressive across the board. I learned an interesting lesson. You have to dig as deep and as hard to unearth good news stories as bad news stories in a company. And the people in the business were smart, hardworking and effective.

Then a man called Bill did something odd. Bill Johnson, who I never met, was Chairman and CEO of the company based in Pittsburgh. He joined Heinz in 1982 and became CEO in 1998. People who worked with him described him as very intense (worrying word 'intense').

Bill had an idea to accelerate growth and usage of one of Heinz's icon brands – tomato ketchup. It was to introduce colour variants – blue, green and pink – to make the ketchup more fun for kids.

When I found out about it I asked who was going to tell him this was a terrible idea, one which would damage the brand and which wouldn't work. It wasn't like that in Heinz, I was told. If Bill said do it, it got done. I'd been brought up in post-Jarrow Britain and disagreed.

But the lunatic colours were launched and crashed to earth, never to be mentioned again.

Lesson: Don't mess with history and icons (remember New Coca-Cola?) and don't make decisions from the top where debate and shared thinking is disallowed. Yes, I'd even apply that to Apple.

When Coca-Cola decided Sidcup was fine

Dasani (Coke's answer to Pepsi's Aquafina) was launched in the USA in 1999. It was Coke's version of a pure bottled water like Perrier, Highland Spring and the others. Rolled out to Canada and South America in 2004, Dasani came to the UK. A number of things went wrong. I'll start again. Everything that could go wrong went wrong.

The product launch was labelled a 'PR catastrophe' as early advertisements called Dasani 'bottled spunk'. (Apparently 'spunk' just means courage in America but in Britain it was a big, messy own goal.) Prior to the launch, an article in *The Grocer*, the trade magazine mentioned that the source of the Dasani brand water was in fact treated tap water from Sidcup. This led to a Food Standards Agency investigation. And this turned out fine... but the damage was done and the media started mocking Dasani as a Del Boy product that was a con job. It gets worse. The UK authorities found a concentration of bromate, a suspected human carcinogen, in the product that could be considered harmful if consumed in very large quantities. Plans to roll out to Continental Europe were ditched. As the 2012 Summer Olympics approached, Coca-Cola (the official drink sponsor) decided not to reintroduce the Dasani brand to the UK market at all.

Lesson: Don't laugh. Coca-Cola is not generally stupid. But twice in the relatively recent past it has decided not to listen to the people out there and do the power-brand thing regardless. One questions whether its PR advisors were asleep or drunk or what. But imagine anything in your life when something goes wrong and then one thing leads to another and another... . The decision to bluff it out was the worst and most expensive of all once the satirical press got going. Cut your losses early.

The master of disintegration?

This is not another 'Fred Goodwin was an idiot' piece. It's about the mythology created around RBS, not least by leading academics from Harvard. 'Masters of Integration' was how RBS was described in the *Harvard Business Review* in 2003 by Nitin Nohria and James Weber. Their article describes the acquisition of NatWest by Royal Bank of Scotland, the strategic rationale for the acquisition and the process by which the integration of the two banks was accomplished. They said that this acquisition was remarkable in its success, given the typically high rate of failure of similar acquisitions. It was, the authors suggested, a model for successfully implementing mergers and acquisitions.

By 2013 Linda Gratton, in the same publication, had a different and more personal take on RBS, viewing the bank through a hindsight lens her colleagues had previously not had available:

'At RBS, CEO Fred Goodwin isolated himself from his colleagues, failed to listen to others, and became increasingly selfish in his behaviour.'

What is more instructive is the reputation RBS had earned not least because of the 2003 article which followed Goodwin being named Forbes Businessman of the year in 2002. From 2003 to 2006 RBS was voted No.1 in Scotland on Sunday's Power 100. As late as 2008 the CEO, Goodwin, was being rewarded for his work by those supposedly in the know, the London Business School making him an honorary fellow.

The fact is that RBS was lauded for its performance. And, as 2008 developed, the urge to do more by media, shareholders, government and the board must have been intoxicating. The bank as a whole became locked in its own 'reputation bubble'. Walking away from ABN Amro would have seemed like cowardice. As Chuck Prince at Citigroup might have said, the music was playing and RBS was enthusiastically asked to keep dancing, never having put a foot wrong for the whole of Fred Goodwin's time there.

Lesson: Don't believe your own reviews. Don't try and learn from your successes. Surround yourself with cheerful sceptics who keep you on your decision-making toes. Beware the real current context changing and remember J.M. Keynes: 'When circumstances change I change my mind. What do you do?'

 **recap**

Lesson 1 – Don't base today's decision on yesterday's success without thinking hard.

Lesson 2 – The consumer often has a stronger sense of a brand's history than its owners and would make better decisions if asked nicely.

Lesson 3 – Look at your feet. Yes they are made of clay – even when you are Coca-Cola or Apple. No one is beyond failing.

Lesson 4 – Don't believe your own media, good or bad. Decide based on evidence, not on rumour.

Notes

1   Jean Buridan (14th century) was a French priest who sowed the seeds of the Copernican revolution in Europe and who was satirised in this paradox by unknown teasers. The paradox had been earlier ridiculed by Aristotle in 350 BC using a man not an ass as the dithering decision-maker.

2   Benjamin Libet, who died in 2007 aged 91, was a pioneering scientist in the field of human consciousness. He was a researcher in the physiology department of the University of California,

San Francisco. In 2003, he was the first recipient of the Virtual Nobel Prize in Psychology from the University of Klagenfurt, 'for his pioneering achievements in the experimental investigation of consciousness, initiation of action, and free will'.

3   Cognosis was founded in 1998 by Richard Brown and Michael Laird, who as clients at Diageo pioneered new planning approaches in the international drinks industry. Today Cognosis is a mid-size strategy firm which in its major research project 'Edge' has reframed the debate about how strategy really works. Their work on leadership, change and strategy is mould breaking.

4   Leon Kreitzman is the author of *The 24 Hour Society* and the co-author, with Professor Russell Foster FRS, of *Rhythms of Life* and *Seasons of Life*. He's an ex-Director of the Henley Centre and executive at Ford Europe. He specialises in the relationship between biological and social factors in determining human behaviour.

5   Ernst Friedrich 'Fritz' Schumacher (1911–77) was an internationally influential economic thinker, statistician and economist in Britain, serving as Chief Economic Advisor to the UK National Coal Board for two decades. His book *Small is Beautiful* is regarded as one of the 100 most influential books of the past 50 years or so. It preaches decentralisation and humanisation of business. He compellingly demolishes the idea that scale creates efficiency.

6   Sydney Finkelstein is Professor at Tuck School of Business, Dartmouth, USA; Jo Whitehead and Andrew Campbell are Directors of the Strategic Management Centre at Ashridge Business School. *Think Again* is a well written and thoughtful catalogue of 'why did they do that?' mistakes. Reading it should be mandatory for every CEO.

PART 5

Creative
thinking

The power of creativity in business is not about inventing the wheel or inventing the internet (yes, that can happen too, of course, though often if it does it's just by accident), it's really about creating differences that give you an edge over your competitors. Everyone has a profound ingenuity; many want to be creative, few think they can be creative yet many can. Transforming your creative thinking happens more easily for some than others but ideas happen when you look, listen, taste, smell and think. Especially think. You can train your brain to think in colour. You really can be usefully creative if you practise. You can discover your imagination.

CHAPTER 8

What makes creativity so powerful and so exciting

Brilliant facts of life

Before getting excited about becoming a creative thinker we ought to take stock about some realities of life which have a day-to-day impact on business and creativity:

- **'The only constant in life is change**.' This is what Heraclitus said 2500 years ago and, ironically, nothing's changed since then.

- **Nudges work better than shoves.** The book *Nudge* has been embraced in Whitehall. Because whispers work better than lectures and nudges and prods are more creative and effective than legislation.

- **The big stuff takes time to happen.** Be patient. It takes a long time to build a cathedral.

- **We are prisoners of the familiar.** Most of us get used to the comfortable world we live in.

- **We are very suggestible to gossip and opinion.** Humans want to make a coherent story out of the information they have, the more lurid the better. And the more fun to pass on… 'you'll never believe it but…'.

- **70 per cent of the battle is getting people to pay attention.** Attention is probably the rarest commodity in the world. If you don't get noticed you don't get bought.

- **Most companies don't believe they can make a better product.** Depressing really. Too many accept mediocrity.

But products have to get better if they are to keep relevant. 'New improved' is still a potent catchphrase.

- **'You miss 100 per cent of the shots you don't take.'** Wayne Gretzky, Canadian Hockey star said this. Don't be frightened of rejection. Try things. The worst thing that can happen is you'll learn a lot.

- **Tough issues can't be solved by black and white thinking.** Creative thinking accepts big problems aren't always simple. But creativity is a very sharp tool.

- **Everything gives us the opportunity to be creative**. Go through life looking for better ways to do things. Imagine a smoother, more smiley and happier place. That's real creative thinking, not writing that novel.

'Creativity can make the familiar new and the new familiar.'

Rory Sutherland

Creative thinking can only work if we have the right brief and we understand the context in which the issue exists that we are trying to solve. Beware being told, as the Saatchi & Saatchi motto memorably, rousingly but misleadingly stated, 'nothing is impossible'. Nice thought but not true. But with a bit of creative wit and effort most problems *can* be solved. When you feel you're stuck trying to solve a difficult problem think about these facts of life to get you back to reality.

The power of creativity

Creativity is a game changer. That's why business leaders talk about it with awe and envy. Everyone recognises what happened at Apple between 1997 and 2011 was astounding and the result of creativity. Similarly there was a creative revolution in advertising in the UK in the 1970s leading to so many leading US outfits being taken over by the British. Creativity is powerful.

Here are a series of observations by some very clever people worth thinking about. If nothing else they help fix the magic of creativity as perceived by those we admire:

- 'Imagination is more important than knowledge' (Albert Einstein).

- 'Imagine a company devoid of creativity and you are looking at a place potentially about to die' (Allan Snyder).[1]

- 'When something exceeds our ability to understand how it works it sort of becomes magical' (Sir Jonathan Ive).[2]

- 'Find out how you are different – then be that. That's where the power is' (Dave Trott).[3]

 'Creativity is the last legal way to gain an unfair advantage' (Maurice Saatchi).

But I don't think we should be talking in hushed tones about creativity. What makes creativity in business work is it helps an idea connect with people. The joy of good advertising is that people first of all notice it and then they talk about it. The thrill of a clever idea is it evokes a 'yes of course' response or, as Jonathan Ive suggests, that look of incredulity that appears on your face when someone does a great magic trick. Most of all it's being able to see and put some form around 'another way' of doing something or finding a 'quicker, cheaper and better' solution.

There's one other good thing about creativity. In the first instance it's free.

Understand what creativity is

Creativity is just another thinking muscle. It gets used by all children in their games and stories and then we manage to educate it out of them. But the muscle is still there, just a bit out of use, that's all.

 **tip**

We need to exercise our creative thinking muscle to get it to work.

Most of are frightened of the unknown. Of the blank page, the blank mind, the void. We find it terrifying. Our minds tell us to avoid that void. Yet it's a blank sheet of paper where the fun starts. A blank sheet on which we can think of putting something, something that seemingly comes out of nothing. The art of surprising, of arriving at a solution that we didn't know we wanted but when we see it we realise it's exactly right. It's about getting rid of the bits that get in the way. It's about creating and dramatising a story by adding colour and excitement to it. It's about filling that blank sheet of paper with thoughts and ideas. It's feeling that underused 'thinking muscle' at work and realising that you can learn how to use it again. By the way, Walt Disney got fired from a first job for 'lacking imagination'. Either his employers were stupid or his creative muscle wasn't working that day.

We should realise that in business, ideas are rare and seldom recognised or appreciated when seen. But all of that can change if we want it to. More and more people become mini master chefs cooking the most extraordinarily complex dishes at home ('Sorry it's only an Ottolenghi recipe… .' Sorry? Sorry?!! They are wonderful recipes but definitely not for the faint hearted. Do one of these and that creative muscle is definitely throbbing.) More people are taking up hobbies from DIY to choral singing to knitting to creative writing courses. More people are doing creative stuff outside work. It's time to bring that developing muscle to the workplace, to your colleagues and to allow you and them to appreciate what your business could be, not just what it is.

Quite often a creative idea is provoked by noticing a discontinuity or a change in behaviour or attitude, something that makes you wonder why a situation's a bit different or hearing about a customer problem several times so you reach the point of wondering whether fixing it mightn't just be the smart thing to do. Creativity isn't blue sky stuff; creativity is rooted in what's going on here and now in front of us and wondering if we can't find a better way. Creativity always consists of questioning and importantly questioning the way things are and doing them differently. The resourcefulness of the human race comprises an appetite for trying things. Rachel Bell of Shine is responsible for the great line 'paper plans are paper planes'. Don't just plan it; try it. Build a prototype or test a concept.

Creativity also depends on making new connections. It was a creative idea to shift the thinking about Airport Terminal shops from thinking functionally about the money you save on 'duty free' shopping in them, to filling the time you have waiting for your plane by doing some pretty exciting, premium shopping. Connections come by jumping from one market to another. A great example is the story of incubators for babies in Africa. They proved too complex and sophisticated for local labour to fix when they broke down until a creative mind worked out a solution. He noticed local labour was great at fixing their 4×4s so they created incubators out of car parts which worked until they broke down and then got fixed by anyone (lots of people) who knew how to fix a 4×4. Thank you Dave Trott for that one.

Most of all creativity in business is not wacky. Some I know put on a funny 'flowers-in-your-hair' psychedelic voice and say 'let's get creative' which is very silly. Creativity is a strong builders' tea activity. And it works best when it recognises how people's minds work. Get people to use their imaginations and lurking there are all sorts of vivid ideas.

Notes

1   Allan Whitenack Snyder is the director of the Centre for the Mind at the University of Sydney, Australia. He has done breakthrough

work into autism and creativity. He has also explored what it takes to make a champion: 'in my opinion, what makes a champion, and I mean a champion in the broadest sense, is a champion mindset. A champion mindset!'

2   Lord 'Jony' Ive is an English designer and the Senior Vice President of Design at Apple Inc. He is the designer of many of Apple's products, including the iMac, MacBook Air, iPod, iPod Touch, iPhone, iPad. Steve Jobs considered Ive to be his 'spiritual partner at Apple'. Ive is living proof you don't have to be wacky to be creative.

3   David Trott, noted advertising man, creative and author. Founder of several successful agencies. Memorable for campaigns like 'Hello Tosh gotta Toshiba?' and Red Rock Cider. Uncompromising upholder of visible advertising.

CHAPTER 9

Ten ways to become brilliantly creative

Thinking on your feet

I was working on a large multinational conference with the top 200 executives of a company at a two-day offsite in Prague with big staged presentations and breakout sessions; a well organised, heavy bonding and career shaping experience. It was the sort of thing where a marketing director's half-hour presentation with videos, slides, music and flashing lights needs to be a tour de force. In short it needs to be creative.

But here was a sudden catch. A very accomplished presenter of a CEO announced the day before: 'No scripts and no lectern. Walk about, be natural, engage the audience.'

This style of presenting – without a script, having learned your part like an actor – is now commonplace. Working from a carefully drafted speech is history. We have moved into a world of 'thinking on your feet' and improvisation because in this mode it's possible to talk to your audience in a way that's based on you gauging their mood at the time, doing it there and then and not how you'd thought it would be two weeks earlier. Improvisation has been described as 'thinking in flight' and if you have the nerve to try it you find new thoughts and connections come to you while you're on your feet. Understand that mental wandering is our thinking default mode and if you've been thinking about your subject all kinds of ideas will be floating around your head in a disconnected way. Walking a stage can liberate them.

 **tip**

Try walking around to get creative thoughts flowing.

And not just walking on a stage. Walking was what Charles Dickens did when thinking up new plots. He was a genius obsessive though and would routinely walk 20 miles a day allowing him to observe, to create thoughts and to release nervous energy.

The real answer lies with your customers

Creativity isn't there as a decorative thing. It's a tool to use. It potentially gives you an edge and allows you to out-think and win one over on your competitors. Specifically most creative thinking that makes a difference does so because it appeals to or excites your end user, your customer.

So what you must do, and it makes no difference what business you are in, is to read customers' emotions, their problems and their deepest desires.

 **tip**

You must know your customers. They don't always want new things but they always want better things.

'There's nothing new under the sun but there's always a better way,' said ad man Ed McCabe.

Three of the most powerful influences in the last 100 years, the car, the web and the pill, have all made lives different and better. We can travel more easily, communicate and learn better and enjoy our lives without fearing unwanted consequences. Overall our desires are well met. We have greater freedom, we have more choice, we are wealthier, healthier and smarter. We are geared up to being more creative and happier. Yet a lot of people are discontented. Creativity alone can't solve the common dilemma that we do not feel better just by satisfying our desires. A new car doesn't do it. That move to a bigger house fails to excite us quite as we thought it would.

Even when consumers are given what they never dreamed they wanted, when they see the product it's exactly right, like the new iPhone or Galaxy or new Sky Atlantic blockbuster or that new Mulberry handbag. Even with those joys their state of mind has not exactly brightened as it should.

It usually helps to go back to first principles. The key human drivers are:

- **Acquiring things** – well this job is being done perpetually and increasingly. All we know from research and experience shows a bigger bonus is not a gateway to better performance and happiness.

- **Bonding and befriending** – social media helps keep us in touch. Everyone who our daughter knows learned about our new granddaughter within hours (or probably minutes) of her birth. Generations Y, Z, F and younger are brilliant at creating and maintaining their acquaintance base. But is this enough? Are acquaintances as good as friends? (Are soft drinks as good as wine?)

- **Learning** – it's never been easier, thanks to the web, to find things out. Increasingly we find errors on Google but if you want to find something out the web is a pretty good way of doing that. As a source of learning it's limited and superficial but it's a great start.

- **Defending** – findings on this are uniform and explicit. People are very risk and loss averse. They'll defend what they've got beyond anything else. That's why salary reduction and job loss are such fraught subjects. That's why death is such a taboo subject.

These are people's red flag or red thread issues. In being creative the strategies that deal with one or more of these have the greatest chance of success.

Getting rid of the creativity blocks

When it comes to creative thinking most of us get blocked by inner voices asking 'what if?' or posing the question 'just suppose x happens…?' The fear of rejection looms larger than the anticipation of success and so long as it does we are driving our creativity with the handbrake on.

> If all the obstacles to your doing something great were removed what would you do?

And here's the hardest question of all: 'If whatever you decide to do next could not fail what would that be?' The terrifying thing is you have things like 'create world peace' and 'end all disease' to beat and then you wonder whether either of those might have an explosive impact on population growth so terrible that the expression 'be careful what you wish for' would come home to roost rather smugly. Creativity needs a bit of grit in the oyster to achieve really great results. Humans handle perfection uneasily.

In fact most people are lacking in confidence when it comes to creative thinking. They think they are reasonably intelligent but weak at creativity (in self-assessment tests respondents scored themselves at 7 out of 10 for intelligence but only at 4.5 out of 10 for creativity.

In removing the most obvious blocks we have to realise that our brain has a habit of lying to us. In research tests where people are asked to solve a problem involving moving a weight from position A to position B and the answer is to swing the weight on a rope pendulum, an obvious solution once seen, they will deny having had any help to get there despite the questioner brushing the rope and giving strong hints. Yes, I'm sorry but the creative muscle in our head tells great whoppers. It's also a brilliant film editor cutting our memory so our 'honest' recollection of history is (how shall I put it?) especially favourable to us. We are heroes in our own memories. We are tolerant, kind and liberal. By the way if you want to find out what you really are deep down try the 'Implicit Association Test' (**implicit.harvard.edu/**). You may be a little surprised.

Creativity is massively impeded if we meet a cynic. There is a variety of terrible expressions cynics have mastered which act like a right hook on our ability to think lucidly, imaginatively and come up with ideas:

'Well, anyway…', 'in the meantime…', 'mind you…', 'let me think about it'… (that means 'no' in plain English), 'suppose for the sake of argument…', 'with the greatest respect…', 'that's all very well but…'. There are lots more if you could only be bothered to think about it (oops… there's another one.)

> Assumptions stifle creativity; assumptions that our ideas won't meet approval, assumptions that the audience won't laugh; assumptions about the worst.

The stifling also happens in institutionalised bureaucracies where the assumption exists that creativity is a bit flippant and 'not for us'. We also seem to have an amazing ability to forget what we know when we know we know something. Memory fade has the greatest demoralising effect on our ability to have ideas. But don't assume what are called 'senior moments' automatically mean creativity wanes with age. The National Bureau of Economic Research shows that 'over the past century the average age at which individuals produce notable inventions and ideas has increased steadily'. Ken Robinson reflects on the role of grandparents as teachers. In Japan the role of *senpai* (senior mentors) is regarded as essential. And here's some good news for oldies:

- Benjamin Franklin invented bifocals when he was 78.
- Grandma Moses was painting until she was 84.
- James Lovelock was going strong at 94.
- David Bowie had a hit record at 67.
- Warren Buffett was wowing us with his one-liners and acumen aged 83.
- Ida Pollock was still writing erotic novels when she died aged 105 in 2013.

Brilliant conditions for creativity

Here are some ways you can improve your creativity.

Be in the right mood

Let your self-esteem roam free. We so often get negative and think the worst of our talents. With few exceptions people have strengths. If only they concentrated on these rather than lamenting their weaknesses they'd be happier and capable of having great 'why don't we?' creative ideas. Cordelia Fine (the psychologist) who has a fine touch with high prose has a belief in the brain's capacity to perform like a confident actor and she said: 'Illusions keep your head high and your heart out of your boots.' And if a measure of self- esteem is an ability to pun my response to that is ... fine. Sydney Finkelstein (Professor in Leadership) takes a more pragmatic view based on years of research:

'When we are and feel in a good mental state,
emotional intelligence and intellectual ability rise.'

Be a bit rebellious

Creativity thrives in a climate of scepticism, when you are in
a questioning mood and when you are up for changing the
status quo. Think about Apple for a moment. Its advertisements
championed misfits, rebels and troublemakers. Now I'm not
advocating growing a beard and putting on battle fatigues – my
kind of rebellion has a sense of humour and is a source of positive energy. It's a rebellion against committee think; against being
dull and boring; and against caution because the cost of caution
is often higher than the cost of making a mistake. Brands like
Snapple, Innocent, Green and Black's, Pret A Manger, North
Face and so on started with and derived their original energy
through kicking back against the boring norm. Some companies
like W.L. Gore and Orvis manage to maintain that 'outside the
bureaucratic box' attitude.

 **tip**

Being a rebel means being your own person and retaining your
ability to think for yourself.

It's no surprise, perhaps, that one of the most inward looking
and cautious executives I met worked for Kodak where I suspect
any kind of rebelliousness would not have been tolerated. Saying
'no' when instructed to do the impossible is rebellious but it's
necessary. Saying 'How about working around this stupid corporate rule?' is guerrilla rebellion but it's necessary. Revelling in the
joy of discovery is the reward for the rebel. Great scientists, the
architects of discovery, are often rebellious because it's arguably
in their DNA.

In his book *The Scientist as Rebel* Freeman J. Dyson says:

'From Galileo to today's amateur astronomers, scientists have been rebels. Like artists and poets, they are free spirits who resist the restrictions their cultures impose on them. In their pursuit of nature's truths, they are guided as much by imagination as by reason, and their greatest theories have the uniqueness and beauty of great works of art.'

Ignite your creative mind

You wouldn't (or shouldn't) play golf without warming up, or run a race without stretching and doing what runners do, or make a speech without wetting your dry lips and getting your mind focused and in the right place.

brilliant tip

Get the juices flowing through, let your mind wander, walk around the problem in your mind and think in 'human' not business jargon.

After your warm-up or ignition you get an 'aha!' moment and you always get this by your unconscious self getting to work. I'm a little suspicious of the 'aha!' moments as for most of us they happen rarely. I'll settle for the 'hmm… hmmm' moment when light begins to dawn and the candle of creativity flicker-ingly comes alight. The essence of creativity is building up little mental structures and then knocking them down again. Think about a young child building with toy bricks – that's what I mean. And as we build our creativity we need to simplify the brief by breaking it into bits. Remember what Henry Ford said; in between designing and building motor cars he had some good thoughts too:

'There's no problem that can't be solved if you break it down into small enough pieces.'

Don't follow the herd

Apple used 'think different' as an advertising strapline in an era when computers were dull like Dell, and Bill Gates was as close to a rock star as you got in business. Anyone in advertising fully understands the need to zig whilst others zag because, apart from anything else, that's how you stand out. But there's more to it than that. Thinking differently is the way you discover new ideas. We live in curiously conformist times with less original thinking than for a long time. Blame perhaps the homogenising effect social media has on behaviour. By blurting onto a 140-character template everyone ends up sounding the same. And there's so much to choose from. There's so much information. So I love this from the late Jerome Weisner, President of the Massachusetts Institute of Technology, who immortally said: 'You cannot drink from a fire-hose.' To gain competitive advantage and out think others, work on the unexpected and be a bit surprising.

'If everybody's thinking alike then someone isn't thinking.'

General Patton

Have fun

My problem with the TV series *Mad Men* is that having worked in that industry myself I thought it had been a lot more fun than Don, Peggy, Joan and Roger seem to have.

 **tip**

Having fun is not irresponsible, it's a creative productivity tool.

When I visited Google's European HQ in Zurich I was struck by an almost institutionalised sense of fun from the fireman's pole joining first and ground floor, the games room, the chill-out room with fish tanks and a bath full of blue foam balls for executives to lie in, the free Lindt chocolate, Ben and Jerry ice-cream and Coca-Cola.

Here's how Janet Lowe describes it in her book *Google Speaks*:

'*The values that drive Google's founders… have created a culture that fosters creativity and fun… '*.

The relation between creativity and laughter is a close one because things that make us laugh the most and are the ones we remember are, like the best ads, often the funniest ones.

A great example of fun with a creative practicality lies in 826 Valencia.[1] That's the number of a shop in a street in San Francisco. Dave Eggers, an author, had made some money from writing a book. With it he decided to set up a creative writing club for children. And he found the premises – 826 Valencia. The trouble was he couldn't get permission for change of use. 826 Valencia had to remain a retail site. So Dave thought a bit and thought creatively. He turned the frontage into a small pirate shop selling stuffed parrots, peg legs, pieces of eight, pirate rum, cutlasses and so on. It had a small door which led to the writing club – 'treasure through here!' Dave turned a problem into a bit of creative fun and a completely satisfying solution. Best of all it's been a thundering success attracting the attention of educationalists and politicians all over the world.

The greatest creative art is simplifying

'Less is more' or it should be because too much information confuses and what we once thought was a good thing, lots of knobs on machines, more and more functions, has turned out to be unstylish and distracting.

 **tip**

> The most fashionable and creative thing to do is take functions away. But it's not always that easy to discard and minimise.

As any whisky brand owner will tell you the process of distilling and then leaving a single malt to mature requires vast patience. Simplification is seen at its potent best in, for instance, Picasso's *Femme* – a few lines telling a whole story – or in a haiku, the verse form described as drops of poetic essence. Here's one by Matsuo Basho written in the 17th century (here loosely translated):

The butterfly perfuming its wings fans the orchid.

If you want to buy anything, doing so on Amazon is so simple. Think like a customer who when she's chosen an item wants to click and go. Or in the case of John Lewis, click and collect (at our local Waitrose). Simples. Or increasingly banking online or at an ATM where a couple of clicks transfers your money between accounts. Again, simples.

Life used to be full of instructions that required you to have a PhD in engineering and linguistics (because they weren't written in English). Increasingly they are shorter, simpler and even intuitive.

But you need to be prolific as an ideas generator

In creativity at its outset, quite simply, more is more. When you are looking for ideas the greater the flow the more likely you'll build on an idea or connect two disparate ones to create something interesting. At the initial stage the editor in your head, the sceptical critic who's saying 'that won't work… that's just silly… it's been done before' needs to be tied up, blindfolded and muzzled.

'The only way to have good ideas is to have lots of ideas.'

Linus Pauling[2]

You need a big pad or a whiteboard and aim to fill it. Scribble what comes into your head. Encourage your creative mind to blurt out anything and everything. You want a 'brain burst' of thoughts not a 'drizzle' of ideas.

The other thing is creativity is a bit like a virus. It's contagious so others will catch it too. A roomful of people unafraid to let it all hang out can be incredibly inspiring. Just keep the ideas coming. As regards how valid these ideas are Kahneman and others in research have shown that the more familiar something is, the truer it is believed to be. This would mean a rumour or urban myth repeated from a variety of sources gains in credibility the more it comes up. It follows that the more a theme recurs in the creative brain burst the more there may be something to it. Jealously guard the key strands of thought in your downloading of ideas in case there's a special gap or need that's being identified.

brilliant tip

Don't be precious: don't be frightened of your ideas being rejected. Good ideas as well as bad ones hit the dust all the time.

Dave Trott reckons that even amongst the most talented advertising men between the various approval processes of research, account management intervention, planners' thinking, management caution and then the client deciding, it takes the creation of 64 good ads to get four good ads to run. It's only the ideas you actually have and present that can be accepted and you'd better have at least 16 before one is statistically likely to run. And now you know why ad men look so stressed.

Storytelling is the greatest creative technique

Desire for the story starts when we are very young. *The Gruffalo*; *The Hungry Caterpillar*; *Peppa Pig*; *Spot*; *Horrid Henry*. Great stories that are page turners you want to hear again and again. Years ago storytelling was in the great hall around the fire listening to the tales of Beowulf or more recently the gruesome story of Sweeney Todd ('Attend the tale of Sweeney Todd...'). So gather round and listen. Stories touch us deeply in our subconscious and we like them.

Too often in business we don't think in terms of narrative but in lists. That's what makes the thud, thud, thud of bullet points so hostile to many of us. Steve Jobs, amongst other things, reinvented the narrative presentation in his launches of new products. TED presentations are 18-minute stories. Thus Sal Khan tells the story of his formation of the online Sal Academy starting with his being filmed by his cousins and put on You Tube ('I realised my cousins preferred to see me on You Tube than in person').

If you aren't used to thinking up stories it really is this simple:

- **What's it all about?** Just say: 'This is the story of a problem we had in trying to fix whatever ... .'
- **Why does it matter?** 'And this was a problem that really upset our customers because whatever ... .'

- **So what did we do?** 'We asked lots of people and did x, y, z and came up with this simple solution... .'

- **And what happened?** 'It didn't work – in fact it was a disaster so we went back to the drawing board and we were drinking our tea when I knocked the mug over and that gave us the idea... whatever.'

- **And did it work?** 'Yes, it worked and the problem is no more... here's what people said about the solution... and I need a new mug.'

 action

set-up → problem → problem worsens → impossible to solve → surprising discovery → solution → everyone happy

In stories we can turn things on their heads. We can see how ideas work in different markets. We can surprise people. But most of all we can engage them. But we need to beware of the drama getting in the way of the truth. Misinformation is our brain's way of retelling a story and editing it so as to reinforce its magic-ness. It's better and more fun to tell but not nearly so useful a business tool.

Just tell stories: don't tell porkies.

Making the stories more magical

Creativity of thinking involves making connections, having leaps of speculative thought and having lots of thoughts. It involves possibly putting two things together no one's done before, like the bladeless fan that Dyson created. In our wilder dreams we really want to know how to create a magic reaction and imagine the impossible (like having your favourite programme that you forgot to record there waiting for you anyway... thank you iPlayer). Or we want to envisage the massively improved (imagine a kitchen slave doing the job you hate the most... thank you dishwasher).[3]

 **tip**

The most striking magic is in the sheer unpredictability of life.

In *The Trouble Shooters*, a TV series featuring Sir John Harvey-Jones[4] in 1990, genial John had a set-to with the very conservative Morgan family, maker of Morgan cars, and predicted the demise of the company unless they took his advice. They didn't. Morgan is still going strong, selling around 700 cars a year with a two-year waiting list. The magic of Morgan beat the logic of John. Morgan aren't selling cars, they're selling escapist fun. They're rather like Harley-Davidsons: the urban myth is that the prime purchasers of these bikes are accountants whose deepest wish is to dress up in leather and ride around frightening people. It's probably not true but I want to believe it is.

 **tip**

Write an FT article about your company and its achievements dated 10 years from now. You'll be amazed at how creative you are – just let your hair down.

Sleights of Mind[5] is a book about magic and the brain. It's written by two psychologists who wanted to discover how easy or hard it is to fool us. The story behind magic, when they deconstruct illusion after illusion, proves that if a mentalist has you in their clutches you can kiss goodbye to free will. They also show how frail our equipment is when faced with a con man. We have a low resolution camera (our eyes); erratic recording device (our memory); lazy brain (constantly presuming what comes next, not observing if it does). It reminds me of that line (slightly mis-quoted) from Viv Stanshall of the Bonzo Dog Doo-Dah Band: 'Let's face it – we're credulous as hell.'

The magic of some stories is that you are living in the middle of them and can't see the wood for the trees let alone (given it's a story) that the Butler did it. In this case the 'Butler' is the Michelin Guide. Michelin launched it in 1900 as a free promotional offer which was designed to get people to drive more and – I can hear the 'creative' in the agency – 'it will allow you to own the highway and become synonymous with the good driving experience'.

In other words, it was transport focused and contained as much on garages as it did on restaurants. It truly was the ultimate driving guide. But something happened. Quite simply the magic of food was greater than the functionality of tyres. And it wasn't until Michelin was about to ditch its expensive promotional idea that it realised what it had. In 1920 Michelin set up a publishing division and started charging for its guide and the rest is history. Michelin stars a century later are the ultimate accolade for great food.

* Good food

** Worth a detour

*** Worth a special journey

The magic of Michelin was it had a great idea and the greatness of the idea was different to that originally conceived.

 tip

Brilliant ideas sometimes get used in quite unexpected ways.

The art of great presentation is the source of creative marketing

I believe in marketing. It has been one of the most effective and entertaining tools of modern business. It not only works; it also makes the world a better place. Selfridges is not a vulgar temple of capitalism. It's a showcase for the best, most creative consumer products that mankind has come up with. Quite simply, it's fun and it's fun done well.

> Experiments psychologists have done show things that are presented well, physically or in words, are enhanced as to how they are perceived as products.

Thus the operation that's 10 per cent likely to kill you or 90 per cent likely to let you live is, in its latter format, an example of more persuasive presentation. Similarly the monetary incentive presented in a big blue envelope is the one people want. If what I've learned about the human brain has led to one finding that's really relevant to business it's this: great presentation is enjoyed and preferred by the average human. The way in which things are presented tells a creative story which makes buying them rather richer than just a transactional experience.

When trying to get children to do what you want and they piercingly ask 'why?' and you find yourself edging towards that uselessly totalitarian 'because I said so' riposte think of marketing. Jonathan Haidt tells the story of presentation with his children and the different response he got from 'you must' and 'can you?' He particularly relished the negative response to 'you musts' even when he completed the sentence 'you must have a lovely ice cream' to be met by 'I shan't'.

We all recognise the need to sell decisions to employees. We just don't do it very well or very carefully. How to package and present management thinking isn't a way of misleading people, it's a way of helping them hear what you have to share with them and making them more positively responsive to their message.

 brilliant tip

Spending time creatively thinking how to make plans look thought through, clear and appealing is time very well spent.

Robert Kennedy – those who knew him speak in awe of his smartness – said something which I find inspiring but which also defines what creativity in words can do. He could have said this in terser, tighter more functional terms but he chose to wrap up the thought in deliciously balanced prose.

Try this brilliant quote:

'There are those who look at things the way they are and ask "why?" I dream of things that never were and ask "why not?"'

Notes

1   826 Valencia was founded in 2002 by author Dave Eggers. The pirate supply store partially funds the creative writing programmes and two satellite classrooms in nearby middle schools. Over 1400 volunteers, including published authors, magazine founders, SAT-course instructors, and documentary filmmakers, have donated their time to work with thousands of students. This has led to several more of these being set up in the USA and one in Hoxton created by Nick Hornby called the 'Ministry of Stories'

where you have to go through a monster shop styled 'Monster Supplies, Purveyor of Quality Goods for Monsters of Every Kind'. This includes 'monster snot'. Lovely.

2   Linus Carl Pauling (1901–94) was an American chemist, biochemist, peace activist and author. He was one of the most important scientists of the 20th century, being one of the founders of the fields of quantum chemistry and molecular biology. He was awarded the Nobel Prize in Chemistry in 1954 and the Nobel Peace Prize for his work on peace activism in 1962. This makes him the only person to be awarded two unshared Nobel Prizes.

3   The first reliable (hand-powered) dishwasher was invented in 1887. The first modern dishwasher incorporating most of the design elements that feature in the models of today was introduced in 1924. Drying elements were even added in 1940. It came at a time when permanent plumbing and running water in the house was increasingly common. But dishwashers were only successfully sold as domestic utilities in the 1950s, albeit only to the wealthy. By the 1970s dishwashers had become commonplace in domestic residences in North America and Western Europe. By 2012, over 75 per cent of homes in the USA and Germany had dishwashers.

4   Sir John Harvey-Jones MBE (1924–2008) was an English businessman. He was the chairman of Imperial Chemical Industries from 1982 to 1987. He became Chairman of the *Economist* in 1989. He was the most famous and acceptable face of British business for two decades.

5   *Sleights of Mind* is written by Stephen Macknik and Susana Martinez-Conde. They are respectively the Directors of the Laboratories for Behavioral Neuropsychology and Visual Neuroscience at the Barrow Neurological Institute, Phoenix, Arizona. They are married and have created the study of 'neuromagic'. It's essential reading but also good fun.

CHAPTER 10

Exercises to help you become creative

tart by thinking about what you want to solve not about just being clever. Creativity is a tool not a goal. If you use the word ingenuity instead and focus on improving things you'll become a lot more grounded.

'There's nothing new under the sun but there's always a better way.'

Ed McCabe

There are those of us who find the word 'creativity' as in the expression, 'well let's be creative about this' difficult. Indeed it's as hard to imagine being creative as being told to 'paint a great picture' or 'sing beautifully'. It will take more than a few well-chosen words to get us in the creative groove. It needs a step-by-step guide to get us going. Let's start at the beginning.

 **tip**

Get the brief right. If you don't you'll be travelling to the wrong place.

Why the brief matters

Get the brief slightly wrong and the solution will be wrong – every time. Unless you say where the destination is (say Manchester) you won't get there, however creative the journey on which you embark. It's that simple. (Unless, of course, you like the surprise of arriving in Marrakesh instead.)

What is a brief?

It's a simple clear directive which identifies the problem and what the solution is designed to achieve.

It also needs to define who the stakeholders are who need to be covered off.

And the context of the problem. It's no use saying later – 'this one was very political because we'd already failed to solve it three times before amid a lot of rancour'.

Ask the right questions to get the right answers

- What is the issue that needs solving?
- Why is this issue a particular problem?
- What would happen if it were solved?
- What would happen if it were not solved?
- Has it been going on for a long time?
- What is the story of the people near to the issue?
- What are the main obstacles to solving it?
- Who cares most about this issue and why?

The key elements step by step

When Henry Ford made his comment about breaking a problem down into smaller pieces he was suggesting something we all agree with but too few of us do. Here's a simple checklist which may help provide an 'interrogation template'. Twenty question areas to help you think. Because the more you think, the more you'll think creatively.

1. People

The most important and difficult factor in any organisation is its people. Great people can make an organisation rock and succeed but, if they are so inclined, they can also bring it to its knees. Professor Ben Bryant[1] of IMD (the International Institute for Management Development in Lausanne, Switzerland) said: 'It's insanity to try and achieve alignment in a business because people are different.'

 **action**

You are dealing with lots of different opinions when you deal with people. How do you get the most out of each of them?

Ask yourself how you can engage them and get them to respond to you. How, in short, do you excite them? How do you create a climate of excellence with which they identify? How do you get them to do great stuff not just talk about it? The big question though is always this one: *'What do they really think?'*

2. Processes

Do the processes which are attached to the issue being examined work? Mazda Cars, based in Hiroshima in Japan, operated a very tight 'just-in-time' process with its parts holding just under a day's stock. In Hiroshima they have hurricanes. I asked what effect this had if the trucks carrying spare parts couldn't get through. The answer? 'We stop the line and everyone sets to tidying and redecorating the factory.' Hurricanes were a godsend to hygiene and efficiency. Look at your processes. Ask if there's a creative way to make them work better. If you were starting from scratch would they be like they are currently?

 **tip**

> Create your own hurricane. Blow away routine. Shake things up to make them better.

3. Products

Are your products good enough? It's an obvious question that isn't asked enough especially as most people think there's not much they can do to change or improve their product anyway. In the late 1980s, when tastes were rather less sophisticated than they are now, Weight Watchers from Heinz introduced a range of Ready Prepared Frozen Meals. To its surprise its Salmon Mornay variety was far and away the best seller. But it was also by far the best tasting and most distinctive product in the range. I wonder if that was why?

 **tip**

> Most business successes come from a better product; most business failures come from product inferiority.

Our use of creativity comes in determining how our product could be better. Could it be better value for money? Could it be cheaper or could we get paid more for it by using better ingredients? Could we do to our product what Apple believed it did to the Mac OS X's user interface: 'We made the buttons on the screen look so good that you want to lick them.' Do you want to lick your product – honestly?

4. Product portfolio

Do you have too many products? Can you simplify your offering and increase your profit? Mothercare, in its peak in the 1970s when it was run by Selim Zilkha just after going public, ran a brilliantly focused operation with a restricted number of stock-keeping units. To get a listing you had to be creative enough to get something else out. Editing is a creative business. It's easier to retain than discard. But the expression 'less is more' really is true.

 **tip**

> Focus your creative attention on fewer things that are great rather than just on lots of things just because they are there.

A less is more story that hit the headlines in the USA was from a young person who worked out that the US Government could save a fortune in printing ink by changing its default typeface from Times Roman to Garamond. I've told you before. Less is more.

5. Positioning

Is what you're telling people about your brand or about your business really compelling? It's easy to be prosaic but does what you say get to the root of your passion and the reason for your brand's existence?

brilliant tip

> Find something true and exciting to tell about your brand. People love inspiring stories.

British Airways had that wonderfully proud claim that was based on fact and which transformed the way the staff felt and accordingly, then, how they treated us – 'the world's favourite airline'. Victor Kiam did it with Remington – 'I liked it so much

I bought the company' – and to a world that didn't know that Audi was German and that in particular it was a product of the best German engineering – 'Vorsprung durch technik'. This was created by advertising agency Bartle Bogle Hegarty 32 years ago. Proof that good creativity can endure.

6. Presence

This is about having stature with those who matter most to you. Ask how you could increase your share of mind with your customers and potential customers. If you are a relatively small brand, like Farrow & Ball, you achieve your presence by impressing a relatively small niche. But Farrow & Ball has progressed from 'who are they?' to market leader of the middle-class mind through creative marketing and brilliant colours. Who else has three shades of black? Suddenly, following the trend, brands like Little Greene, Benjamin Moore's Aura and Dutch Boy have emerged.

> Creativity is catching. Markets take off when competitors start spreading the creativity virus and catching ideas from each other.

7. Promoting what and how?

All that money spent on marketing... go on, ask the question – is it working? The argument is that 'creative' saves money because it gets noticed and attention is the hardest thing of all to command. How do you find out what matters to your most loyal core customers? Do what Stuart Rose did when he joined M&S – he talked to Women's Institutes and asked them 'what do you think?' Those WI members gave him some pretty pointed opinions and ideas.

 **tip**

Spend your money on promotion only when you know your most influential champions are tuned in to it and on your side.

If you are trying to judge a campaign for tourism talk to taxi drivers – how good the promotional campaign is will affect their wallets and be reflected in what they say to you.

8. Channels of distribution

Could you transform your business by changing your route to market. Would you be better off selling direct? Think about your end users and how you might get to them more effectively and more profitably.

Direct Line, the motor insurer, was the pioneer of selling insurance direct and as broker-driven insurance got more expensive people discovered Direct Line gave a better service and saved them money.

9. Pricing

The whole area of pricing is complex. We can live in a society where premium priced grocery does well and cut price grocery does well and all the players in the middle get a bit hurt. Ask the questions: do your main users think you are price competitive? Should you try dynamic pricing?

 **tip**

Price promote noisily so it makes a real difference (if it doesn't make a difference you're just giving margin away).

Alternatively, should you be premium priced so it makes the right statement about your brand? The factory direct malls in the USA in places like Manchester, Vermont work brilliantly because you get luxury brands half price but when you go to Bergdorf Goodman in New York City you get the real experience of luxury and you feel rich. Even when you get the bill!

10. Structures

Do you have the right internal structures? Is it clear who does what? Is accountability defined properly? Are you as lean as you could be? At GE they reckoned the key roles you had to get right were CEO (leadership); CFO (money); Head of HR (people).

 **tip**

> Most businesses have too many people and they only discover just how bad it is when the bad times come.

Can you be creative in defining roles? I heard of an HR Director called 'Casting Director' – what a great way of redefining that role. And remember 'less is more'. Do you really need to do all the things you do with all those people required to do them?

11. Culture

A business devoid of a distinctive culture will never be a great business. When Professor Chris Bones[2] was asked why RBS had gone so wrong, he talked about the lack of values in the business. I'm not sure there were no values but the constant process of acquisition and the way people were driven was, at the very least, culturally divisive.

 **tip**

Your business will be a product of what it does, what makes it different and what passion drives it. This is its 'culture'. Treasure it. It characterises your organisation.

Great cultures are seen (like it or not) at Ryan Air, John Lewis, Pret A Manger, Aldi, Jordan's and in smaller businesses like Daunts Books in Marylebone and Hampstead or Nicole Urbanski in Hove.

12. Strategy

Do you know where you want to go and what you want to be? Can you write this down in a single sentence? Great strategies are those like Aldi's; like Green and Black's; like Warburtons; and like BMW's. And having defined where you want to go and what you want to be, can you clearly describe how you plan to get there. Freek Vermeulen[3] is entertainingly critical of modern management. Read this:

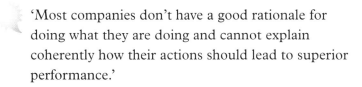 'Most companies don't have a good rationale for doing what they are doing and cannot explain coherently how their actions should lead to superior performance.'

Ask these questions:

- Are we making choices or are we creating a catch-all strategy?
- Are we stuck in the status quo?
- Are we looking to create value or just sell stuff?
- Is our strategy a secret kept only in the boardroom?

13. Tactics

How good is this business at execution? However good the menu may look, how good is the food and the service in this restaurant? How good is it at making things happen? John Westerby writing in the *Times* put it rather well:

 'Good ideas are common; what's uncommon is someone who will work hard enough to bring them about.'

It's instructive just walking around a business and watching what people do (or quite often don't do). To see people looking as though they really know what they are doing watch football or rugby teams like Real Madrid or New Zealand at work. Alternatively do what I did. I went up the Shard at London Bridge as it was being built. It's 87 storeys high, a complex planning feat and was completed in just three years – again a tribute to the brilliant execution we achieve in civil engineering in the UK. It was the professionalism even more than the building that was awesome. But it was the creativity involved in the execution that blew me away. They practised the assembly of the steel structure on the top with the complete team on a disued airfield so step by painstaking step everyone knew exactly what they were doing. 'A military exercise?' asked a colleague. 'No, like rehearsing a ballet' came the answer.

14. Leadership

Are you well led, inspiringly led and strongly led? Leaders need to be great, inspiring communicators like Justin King, ex CEO of Sainsbury's or Charlie Mayfield of John Lewis. To lead, you have to lead change and make people want to follow you. You have to accept that there may be a better way of doing things and actively seek it. Yet generally the biggest block to creativity comes from the top. Freek Vermeulen sounding off again says:

'Business leaders believe that because everybody had always done it this way, it is the best way of doing things.'

 **tip**

> Leaders can make a huge impact by behaving creatively. Think how to surprise, engage and excite. Suggest holding your next offsite at Alton Towers... be a bit wild.

15. Customers

What do your customers really think about you and what you do? How could you improve this? Do you *really* know what they collectively think that you need to improve or change? Companies like Nestlé, Kellogg, P&G and Heinz really do.

 **tip**

> Engage your trade customers to help you understand your end consumers better. Ask them to be your eyes and ears too.

Are you being creative enough in communicating with your customers and in finding out how their thoughts are developing? When did you last sit and listen to a group of them talking about what they and their customers want?

16. Competitors

Do you know who they are? Do you know what they are better at or worse at than you? Are they improving or changing in any way? Do you know what they think of you?

 **tip**

> Analyse competitors' strengths and aim to match those. Then decide how you can be better in a key way and focus on that.

Tesco told us something really useful. When it really accelerated ahead of Sainsbury's was when it focused on its own performance and articulated and developed its own values. I wonder what its people are saying now.

17. Knowledge

Is there a deep pool of market and customer understanding sitting in the business? Is it readily accessible or is it mislaid, forgotten or archived? In insurance the quality of management information can spell the difference between success and failure. In all businesses I know it's the 'knowledge' that's wasted that seems a crime. The 'knowledge' is the stuff that's been tried and failed and all that insightful, expensive consumer research that's been filed away.

 **tip**

> Don't waste the 'knowledge'. There's creatively inspiring riches here.

18. Momentum

Is there momentum in the business? Does it feel dynamic or inert? Is it full of debate, challenge and change?

 **tip**

> Time to 'get on a roll'. Accelerate the pace in your business and everyone's thinking moves to 'what's new?' mode.

Google are always on the move, always have momentum, going somewhere new and creating, for instance, imaginative partnerships with organisations such as NASA. HBO has momentum – what's the next hot series? Waitrose has momentum. Momentum spells money. When a Waitrose opens near your house your house goes up in value. That says a lot about the brand.

19. What the papers say

Are you keeping up to the mark with what's in the papers, material that you can use or refer to? When the 2014 Sochi Winter Olympics opening firework ceremony had the problem of one of the five Olympic rings failing to open, a viral ad for Audi showing this appeared with the line: 'When four rings is all you need'. (The Audi logo is four rings.) Brilliant. Only Audi claimed that it was nothing to do with them. Even more brilliant when someone else does your work for you.

 **tip**

Are you newsworthy? Are you part of the zeitgeist? When other people advertise you, then you're on a roll.

The news is important so you need to keep up to date with it. What you do and what you sell exists in the real world where lots of things are going on. Try to be part of the creative tide, not just a pebble on the shoreline.

20. So what are the most creative things going on outside your market?

Some of the best creative ideas are ones you can borrow from other markets. How can ideas like the following be used? Tester pots in paint, faster invoicing like the bill delivery at Brasserie

Zedel, free breakfasts for staff, new bright colours in kitchen-ware, newspapers online – all amazing changes. The list is as big as your sense of curiosity. What ideas can you borrow or shamelessly steal?

'Amateurs borrow: professionals steal.'

Picasso

But you could add 'creative people adopt and then adapt'. That's a pretty good definition of pragmatic creativity.

The creative process

Creative thinking in business is not meant to be fancy, it's there to make something change; in short it's a tool not an ornament. Edward de Bono said:

'The logic of creativity is the logic of patterning systems… it can be defined as the search for alternatives.'

So the mood that dictates the process is one where we readily accept change to the status quo, change to 'an alternative state'. Any change like the sudden drop in temperature which we know will happen when we dive into a swimming pool requires courage, stamina and determination.

David Allen[4] gave some very good advice. It's essentially 'get on with it' but he dresses it up much more nicely:

'Taking the first logical step towards completing a task relieves people of much of the worry of things undone and clears the mind to allow creative thinking.'

Disciplined creativity

You will be relieved to hear that the expression 'thinking outside the box' will be used only once in this book and that is here. It is, of course, the commonly used way of describing creative thinking and it's not very helpful. Most of the time what is needed in business is to actually think *within* the box, within the rules that have been set by the consumer or the trade or your own corporate guidelines and within that box to do something that is truly unusual.

If you are in advertising and are asked to do a 48-sheet poster it is generally unhelpful to think of a triangular poster or a round poster. The 48-sheet box is the medium. It's what you do inside it that counts. Even Picasso regarded the confines of the brief to be the challenge and not, in general, the challenge being to write a new brief.

My favourite story about creative thinking that really works – what I am calling 'pragmatic creative thinking' – is from Mick Nash, the Managing Director of Sedley Place, the design company. A friend of his who became a client and a colleague was a schoolteacher who was exasperated by the children in his classes constantly leaning backwards on their chairs and over-balancing. It was disruptive and dangerous. In fact around 5000 children a year go to hospital for treatment after falling over backwards and banging their heads. So he asked Mick, 'Can you solve the problem by designing a chair that can't overbalance when they lean backwards?' Mick said he could. 'Ah,' said his friend, 'but here's the really tricky bit – it has to cost less than £20.'

I love Mick's response.

'That's not the tricky bit. It's actually the brief.'

Things that get the creative juices going

Be 'what makes a champion'

Professor Allan Snyder from Australia and Director of Centre for the Mind makes some interesting observations:

'Thinking of "creativity" as a driving force stresses the power that

many people see in it. Imagine a company devoid of creativity and you are looking at a place potentially about to die. Studies have shown that child prodigies… rarely amount to anything (…with exceptions like Mozart). What is really important is learning how to struggle, how to recover from adversity and how to adapt…. I arranged for Nelson Mandela and a group of 50–60 extraordinary people to be together… what I discovered was that creativity is an act of rebellion….'

 'To be creative, you have to confront conventional wisdom; you have to break with convention.'

Give yourself time

One further point – very often the best companies take a while to mature too. Sam Walton opened his first store in 1945 but took 17 years getting the Walmart model right. His first Walmart opened in 1962 and the next 24 stores opened in the next five years. It was worth waiting for.

 **tip**

We are too impatient. Sometimes getting it right takes trial, error and time.

So what are some of the most important secrets to the conditions in which your creative thinking can flourish?

Be subversive

I went on an offsite in Switzerland with the advertising and marketing group WCRS. We had a series of group creative games at one point. One, facilitated by an American couple who were world famous at this stuff, comprised making as many small white houses as you could in half an hour out of cardboard. Our group revolted because it seemed so silly. We made an enormous house out of white card with white card Ferraris and Porsches in the drive. The facilitators told us we were a disgrace and this had never happened before and said: 'Just wait for it guys, because the other teams will hate you. They will laugh at you.' The reverse happened. Everyone wanted to be in our team. They applauded us. The facilitators were booed and fled the meeting. Creativity 3 – Process 0.

 **tip**

> Be careful. Bend a few rules but don't break hearts or risk breaking the business.

Say what you really think, go with your gut and don't be frightened. If something feels wrong to you then it probably is.

Be relaxed and receptive

Are you really relaxed, attentive and receptive? Are you comfortable in your shoes? Are you excited by the prospect of discovering new things? Are you deeply interested in what's going on around you? Einstein, who is mentioned from time to time in this book (in any book on creativity he has a big share of the market in ideas), said:

'I am neither especially clever nor especially gifted, I am only very, very curious.'

Curiosity is the oxygen of creativity.

Curiosity is also fun.

Be prepared to understand complexity

Paradox and confusion lie at the centre of the modern world so anyone who demands black and white solutions is going to be unhappy. If (as it must be) complexity is to be unravelled then it needs especially open and receptive minds and an ability to juggle thoughts and issues. Complexity leads to creativity because it makes you really use your brain.

But complexity has a particular side-benefit. Because it's hard to get your head round it, if you in fact and by hard work manage to do so, you will have a competitive advantage.

 **tip**

In a knowledge economy it's smart to try and get smarter. A 'that's clever' customer response also wins you sales.

Accept whatever the right one turns out to be

Don't try and bend the evidence to prove your point. The most successful creative thinkers are open-minded and prepared to be very surprised but receptive to whatever answer they might get – even if it's contrary to what they hoped. Dogma and a determination to be right impede being creative. Changing your mind is not a crime but rather, as John Maynard Keynes said earlier, an absolute necessity.

Remember creative thinking will lead you to surprising places. It requires you to be nimble and flexible not dogmatic. That's why it's so powerful: it liberates you from the ordinary.

Be productive because more leads to more choice and even more ideas

Do not be lulled into thinking one idea will do. Lots of ideas give you the chance to think again, select and to refine them. The trouble with having only one idea is it presupposes that you are infallible, which you aren't.

The most modest geniuses I know say they've only had a couple of decent ideas in their life. They underestimate their talent.

In fact they have an endless stream of good thoughts because to have good ideas it's more helpful to start with lots of ideas. Not everyone agrees with this. French academics from L'Ecole Nationale Supérieure des Mines in Paris argued in early 2014 that innovation has little to do with quantity. Insofar as they're sceptical about old fashioned brainstorming I agree but I fear they take a very pure French academic view. And academic innovation is an oxymoron.

Remember that team beats solo

Creativity is seldom a solitary pursuit (except when it comes to maths, writing a book, poetry or composing music… and even then composing solo is arguably not the best or only way).

 **tip**

To create a great business-ideas machine you have to be very skilled at getting the best out of those around you.

Encourage them to be full of 'let's try' and 'could we' and 'what if' (the impressive innovation company based in Marylebone, incidentally, call themselves '!What If?' In its book, *A Creative Revolution at Work*, the authors describe the key to a creative team being to:

'source a wider diet, seek out new experiences and ways of thinking about their market, products and internal processes… the new perspectives they gain provoke them into making creative connections that others won't have made.'

The company launched 'Skinny Innovation' in the recession. It's about being creative on a budgetary diet necessary for the straitened economic times in which we were living; having creative insights demands brain power and team power, not lots of money.

Creative connections are the root of creativity. Here's an interesting example: Yotel, the airport hotel business. Its rooms are designed to be very small but luxurious. It achieved this by asking the designer of British Airways First Class cabins to do the design because it realised he'd understand space limitations brilliantly. Saving space, saving money became the brief.

Make diversity a key to creative thinking

You need to have a mixed group in your team if you are to have thoughts that are truly breakthrough. Here's what G. Pascal Zachary said about diversity in the *Wall Street Journal*:

'Diversity spawns creativity, nourishes the human spirit, spurs economic growth and empowers nations.'

That's terrific because it drills to the core of what makes the human race so adaptable. Research has also shown that a diverse group will always be better at creative problem-solving than a group of like-minded, similar people, however clever they are individually.

Surprise me and make me laugh

Don't underestimate the power of humour, which is why it is one of the most creative tools there is. Most humour relies on a shift in dimension or the creation of a new connection or the simple surprise that an unexpected ending can have. Many jokes like many great inventions or discoveries are so obvious when they are delivered although not foreseen.

Do not underestimate the importance of surprise in creative thinking… the moment when logic seems to go out of the window and a 'creative leap' takes place.

'The great thing about listening to someone with a sense of humour is you listen extra hard in case they say something funny.'

Baroness Trumpington

Visualise and dream

Practise deep imagination and develop the power of visualising what things might be like in different circumstances. Imagining what brand leadership would feel like to your business and your people might lead you to discover what it feels like having a product superior to competition (not a blinding insight to be sure but it might refocus you on to what is needed in your own company). The power of being able to imagine yourself in a different place, experiencing all the sensations of smell and taste and sound and touch and sight is enormously powerful whenever you do it in a day-dream. But you probably do it most nights when you dream at night anyway.

Dreams are even more powerful if you can get them to *work* for you. Just because you are asleep doesn't mean your computer is turned off. Try two things before you go to sleep:

- Put all the issues you are struggling with into a metaphorical box and imagine locking it.
- As you are going off to sleep imagine what it might feel like having solved your problem in a brilliantly creative way. I've tried that and dreamed of the solution. Kekulé[5] dreamed of the structure of both carbon and benzene. Dream on... it works.

If you can't explain it simply, something's wrong

Do not imagine that random, off-the-wall pieces of 'inspiration' will cut any ice with an investor. In creativity there may be leaps and breakthroughs but it can always be explained in the same way an accomplished critic can deconstruct a painting or a poem.

 tip

If a 'creative' idea is inexplicable or illogical it isn't creative, it's silly.

Yet it's the people who aren't very creative who are most likely to be taken in by a piece of crackpot daubing. The very word 'creative' can switch off the critical faculties in some just as 'algebra' can freeze the brains of others. If you're creative-averse don't be hooked by fairy dust. An idea may transcend logic but if it seems daft it probably is daft. Quite often that emperor isn't wearing a set of magic clothes. He's stark naked.

The six enemies of creativity

In life we say 'know thine enemies'. In order to think creatively it's useful to be clear about what factors most get in its way, who the enemies of creativity are. Alternatively if you are an autocratic leader who wants to stamp out creativity here's how to do it.

 tips

Stamping out creative thinking – for good!

Create a state of fear. Given the way some companies are run 'fear' has become a prevalent issue with people looking over their shoulders and worrying about their future (if any). People who are in fear of losing their job or apprehensive about the reaction of their peers, may (wisely) have decided to keep their head down. But this is a rotten posture from which to attempt creative thinking. **Creative enemy rating 5/5**.

Create stress. Having a frisson of adrenalin when you are doing a presentation or are about to do something new and difficult is productive and healthy. However the disabling strain of anxiety brought on by overwork is alien to that calm, receptive and patient feeling that the 'waiting creative mind' should feel. Stress is an enemy to almost anything worthwhile. If you feel it, stop what you are doing... go for a walk, have a conversation, have a beer or anything just to keep it at bay. **Creative enemy rating 4/5.**

Cause distraction. The discipline of creative thinking requires concentration and focus. Don't try and do it whilst fiddling with your iPad because people with short attention spans will seldom be much good as creative thinkers. I believe that multitasking has become a practice so widespread and pernicious that we all need to campaign against it and the myth that it's cool. **Creative enemy rating 3/5 for others and 5/5 for those doing it**.

Show a lack of co-operation. If those around you are frightened of creativity, think it's irrelevant to the spreadsheets they have in front of them or they just don't want to try and think creatively it makes the generation of new ideas really difficult to achieve. But at least you can ignore them. They'd rather be playing on the laptop anyway. **Creative enemy rating 3/5.**

Be actively cynical. But there is one obstacle even worse than passive indifference and that is when you are with a bunch of intelligent people who are scornful about the creative adventure. There is little you can do (in fact just one person with the wrong attitude can stymie you). Given that changing their minds is unlikely and murdering them is an over-extreme option (are you sure it's extreme; it might be the only way?), the best way forward is to politely suggest to the cynics that they leave the team before they make you become a cynic too because cynicism is very infectious. **Creative enemy rating 5/5.**

Be very bureaucratic. Small companies are usually more creative than big ones because they are more focused on ideas. Big companies, with hierarchy and a process way of working, can be anti-open-minded. The bijou perfection of a Ben and Jerry, Prêt a Manger and Innocent were all creative successes and although now sold in total to larger businesses seem to have retained a bit of the rebel in what they do. But if you want to stop creativity, stamp it out, then just set up complex systems, processes and forms to be filled and in no time you'll be creative-free. **Creative enemy rating 4/5**.

A story about creativity

'Stone me, Professor'[6]

A professor stood before his philosophy class and had some items in front of him.

When the class began, he wordlessly picked up a very large and empty mayonnaise jar and proceeded to fill it with golf balls.

He then asked the students if the jar was full.

They agreed that it was.

The professor then picked up a box of pebbles and poured them into the jar. He shook the jar lightly.

The pebbles rolled into the open areas between the golf balls.

He then asked the students again if the jar was full.

They agreed it was.

The professor next picked up a box of sand and poured it into the jar. Of course, the sand filled up everything else.

He asked once more if the jar was full.

The students responded with a unanimous 'yes'.

The professor then produced two beers from under the table and poured the entire contents into the jar effectively filling the empty space between the sand.

The students laughed.

'Now,' said the professor as the laughter subsided, 'I want you to recognise that this jar represents your life. The golf balls are the important things – your family, your children, your health, your friends and your favourite passions – and if everything else was lost and only they remained, your life would still be full.

'The pebbles are the other things that matter like your job, your house and your car.

'The sand is everything else – the small stuff.

'If you put the sand into the jar first,' he continued, 'there is no room for the pebbles or the golf balls.

'The same goes for life.

'If you spend all your time and energy on the small stuff you will never have room for the things that are important to you.

'Pay attention to the things that are critical to your happiness.

'Spend time with your children.

'Spend time with your parents.

'Visit with grandparents.

'Take time to get medical check-ups.

'Take your spouse out to dinner.

'Play another 18 holes.

'There will always be time to clean the house and fix the waste disposal.

'Take care of the golf balls first – the things that really matter. Set your priorities.

'The rest is just sand.'

One of the students raised her hand and inquired what the beer represented.

The professor smiled and said, 'I'm glad you asked. The beer just shows you that no matter how full your life may seem, there's always room for a couple of beers with a friend.'

Notes

1   Ben Bryant is Professor of Leadership and Organisation at IMD before which he was a Fellow of the Centre for Management Development at the London Business School. Amongst other things he has focused on and written about leaders needing to embrace complexity. He's a great lecturer.

2   Chris Bones is Partner and co-owner of Good Growth Ltd. He is also professor of Creativity and Leadership at Manchester Business School and Dean Emeritus at the Henley Business School.

3   Freek Vermeulen is an Associate Professor of Strategy and Entrepreneurship at the London Business School. He writes, consults and speaks across the world on topics such as strategies for growth, strategic innovation and making strategy happen.

4   David Allen is recognised by Forbes as one of the top five executive coaches in the US. *Time* magazine called his flagship book, *Getting Things Done*, 'the definitive business self-help book of the decade.' In it he argues that it is often difficult for individuals to focus on big picture goals. By developing a system that clarifies and defines the regular workday, an individual can free up mental space to begin moving up to the next level of focus.

5   Friedrich August Kekulé 1829–96 was a German organic chemist. From the 1850s until his death, Kekulé was one of the most prominent chemists in Europe, especially in theoretical chemistry. He was the principal founder of the theory of chemical structure. Kekulé's most famous work was on the structure of benzene.

6   This story appears in many places but in none have I found the original source attributed. It seems like one of those urban myths. Do you know who the first Professor was? However the first chapter of *The Now Effect* by Elisha Goldstein, PhD, entitled 'The Wisdom in Golf Balls' contains the story.

CHAPTER 11

Winning strategies for your creative journey

This chapter focuses on exercises and behavioural changes which if tried separately or together can radically uplift your ability to get a flow of ideas. None of them will turn you into a creative thinking genius overnight but some of them may, like Pilates or Yoga, strengthen your core, your core of creativity. They are there to make 'thoughtfulness' second nature rather than something just done by people in advertising agencies.

Because all of us need more good ideas

Where does innovation in business come from? Experience shows it's rooted in attention to detail. It's not simple and it can come from many places, but much of it derives from a culture of people being alert to every aspect of the customer experience. What really matters is being product and service obsessed. The experience of actually using your products and discovering their potential and limitations is what drives and helps refine innovative thinking in most companies.

But we must be careful about making too big a deal about creative thinking. What frightens people off is thinking they'll be asked to create the next Harry Potter novel or the next *Game of Thrones*. If they created a minor interesting character in either that would be astonishing. It would be enough.

 **tip**

A little step forward, a small improvement or a change which makes some lives easier, now that's creative (and it's useful too).

Imagine being asked to increase at a stroke the sales of UK food by 15 million tonnes and you'd struggle to come up with an idea. After all, that would work out at around 1½ lb of food per adult in the UK per day. Per day! (If you believe that number, of course, because Google which is my source can't get it wrong or maybe they can and it seems too large to me… still the principle remains the same.)

Solution: how about introducing sell-by dates?

The mischief-maker in me loves the idea that sell-by dates are a way of driving sales volume. 'Mr Sell-By' is responsible for consuming more food in our house than anyone else. Of course I'm not suggesting their introduction was a cynical marketing idea but we are now throwing away tins and frozen food too. No, it's the idea that we can reduce larder-stock and unblock the pipeline just by someone putting an arbitrary date on a pack. If we had had that idea as a sales idea it would have been very creative… maybe it was.

brilliant **example**

On the basis that everything that exists creates an opportunity for creative thinking how about this? Heinz launched an innovative 'Fridge Pack' for baked beans which can be kept in the fridge for up to five days after opening, giving us longer to eat the product. Snap packs were also developed to give handy, single-person portions.

Someone is still thinking.

Brilliant exercises for getting our minds ready to think creatively

Getting ready

You need to warm up and get in the right 'zone' for creative thinking. Here are some simple preparation exercises so you can make creative thinking easier. All are about getting into a suitably receptive state of mind:

- Have a blank mind – empty it of preconceptions, opinions and biases.
- Be very relaxed – get comfortable, warm, loose clothing and no phone.
- Feel hungry to get something done (not just famished for food).
- Believe you really might enjoy this and that it's going to be useful.

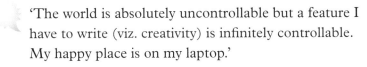

'The world is absolutely uncontrollable but a feature I have to write (viz. creativity) is infinitely controllable. My happy place is on my laptop.'

Caitlin Moran

Try doodling

Something happens when you scribble.

Something happens when you put some random thoughts onto a piece of paper or a screen. Think about a problem you want to solve, something clear like say 'how to increase sales'. Spend 5 minutes loose-doodling:

Sales growth/decline/trends → number of salespeople → spread of achievement → distribution channels → levels of distribution → customer satisfaction → product comparison with competition → pricing → packaging → customer service → after-sales data → why do people buy? → why stay loyal? → is it high on their radar? → which competitor's doing well? → what do people say is going on? → what *is* going on? → is there a big idea lurking unused? → an idea which = biggest, best, cheapest, fastest, slowest, cleverest, easiest, smartest, safest, coolest and so on? → what's the best we can expect as we are? → what's stopping us doing better than that? → imagine a real winning streak → what would that take?

Now just look at that – all those questions – write down what comes to mind; sit and think… just download your thoughts – clear your mind – this will ignite your creative thinking. Doodles can be whatever you want – italic (*doodle*), bold (**doodle**), numeric (123456) or even sort of graphic (R♥K)… just let yourself go.

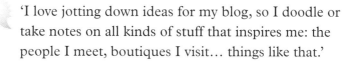

'I love jotting down ideas for my blog, so I doodle or take notes on all kinds of stuff that inspires me: the people I meet, boutiques I visit… things like that.'

Maria Sharapova

Practise deep breathing

Do it for a few minutes trying to loosen up your neck, shoulders and hands. Rub your hands together. Stretch. Or, best of all, take a Pilates class and speak to your body. But if you are a busy person who like me neglects exercise and you feel stressed, just become a regular deep breather; deep breathing is always good for you, as is simply learning to breathe properly. Yoga is supposed to transform the way we breathe, feel and think.

'We breathe to live. Without breath we die.'

Catherine Elizabeth Ward

Increase your energy levels

Carrots provide the quickest release of blood sugars you can achieve. Or if you prefer (because you hate carrots – yes I know raw carrots seem to have hung around rather a long time) try Snickers, a Red Bull or a banana. Creativity needs to be fed with sleep, with energy and with plenty of that 'feel good' sensation. Exploring ways to achieve all three in the best way for you is your mission. I'm less worried about the calories; I'm more worried about the inspiration you'll need and can get. Lean, hungry and grumpy is what we're trying to avoid. So eat and chew your way to ideas. Every mouthful is another creative insight.

Use soft eyes

Relax. Close your eyes. Then open them, stare at nothing spe-cific and let your mind gently wander. This will help you become passively observant. Stare dreamily at a whole scene without focusing on anything in particular. Let things come to you rather than you trying to organise what you see. Enjoy being still, yet still alert. Avoid that fidgety, uneasy state that characterises today's world; flashes of 'I should have done'… or 'what if x happens?' Don't worry; let ideas float into and out of your head.

'The world is ruled by letting things take their course.'

Lao Tsu[1]

I'm not sure this quote is a guaranteed career builder but the principle of letting things come to you sometimes rather than always trying to force the issue resonates strongly. Ideas can be resistant to bullying. And we don't like bullies.

 **tip**

Your senses need to be indulged – favourite taste, happy smells, soft clothes, right light and your favourite creative music – now try thinking ...

Change your mood

What you really want is a mood that's full of brilliant, positive thinking. Musical stimuli can help change the way you feel. These choices will, by the way, depend on your personal taste:

- **Going to a meeting/'we're going to win' music** (for me, mostly from films: *The Magnificent Seven, The Big Country, 633 Squadron, The Great Escape, The Dirty Dozen, Patton,* the friendship duet from Verdi's *Don Carlos,* Beatles' *Eight Days a Week, Lord of the Rings, Pirates of the Caribbean,* Clapton's *Layla,* etc., etc.

- **More reflective music:** *An Officer and a Gentleman,* Carly Simon, *You're So Vain,* anything from Verdi's *La Traviata,* Bernstein's *Somewhere,* Cher's *Gypsies, Tramps and Thieves,* the Friendship Duet from *The Pearl Fishers.*

- **Thinking music:** Mozart. (Sir Paul Robertson, leader of the Medici String Quartet, who also teaches music, has done a lot of work with autistic children and has shown that Mozart's music has a particularly beneficial effect on their behaviour because of its intricate note patterning and how that affects the brain.)

 **tip**

Music is a useful kind of 'psychological glue' which reminds you of what it feels like being where you want to be and of what you stand for.

And now define yourself

While you are about it choose the eight Desert Island Discs that define who *you* think *you* are. In a complicated world which can be quite political, you want to stay true to your values and it's an appealing idea to summarise the real you musically.

Use history to help you change your mood

We live in the present not in the past but what you've done and where you've come from can be helpful in shaping the way you frame your thoughts. This could very easily be said by a teacher or a sports coach: 'Getting into the right frame of mind can be helped by recollecting previous triumphs or moments when you felt in really great form.'

Lose your ego

The two things that most impair creativity are protecting your own particular piece of corporate turf and regarding the exercise as personal ('it's my idea that matters; what's in it for me? am I looking good?') So you need to lose your ego and open your eyes to others. Start by reflecting on the real you.

'Be what you is not what you ain't, 'cos if you ain't what you is, you is what you ain't.'

Luther B. King

By pinning down your core values and being true to yourself you'll get new creative energy. Your ego slows you down because it means you are worrying about how you feel and how others see you.

Ego-busters

It's not easy discarding your ego but try these three tips:

- Assume whatever you think about will not have any effect upon you (good or bad).

- Imagine yourself as an author not a player in the creative exercise on which you are embarking.
- Imagine you have everything you want and you are doing this task for the person you care about most.

Map your influence and experience

Map what you've done, what you know, who you know, the list of the most important influences on you, the most amazing places you've visited, the best things you've done.

Stop being influenced by what others say and think

If people tell you you are wonderful, or not so wonderful, or that you have skills, or that you don't, take it all with a pinch of salt and don't get too fussed by it. Some of the greatest people have been told they aren't going to make it (for example: Robin Cousins the skater by a new coach; and the Beatles by Decca).

Define your single key strength

Yes, I know it's really hard to do this but if by the end of this book you can say any of these:

- 'My key skill is storytelling', or
- 'My major asset is my memory', or
- 'I'm great at drawing ideas out from others',

then if you can do any of those then you will have achieved a huge amount of good. Focus on what actually makes you remarkable... not what you'd like to be good at. This will involve asking others what they think about you.

Break your routine

If we always do everything the same way, how we can we ever expect to achieve anything different? Behaving differently can allow you to see things in a new way.

'Insanity is doing the same thing over and over again and expecting different results.'

Albert Einsten

Change your work routine

Get in late, leave early or get in very early and leave at lunchtime. Try to parcel up work into segments like 'just getting stuff done', 'really making something valuable happen', 'sitting and thinking' and 'having an inspiring productive meeting'.

Just don't let the day drift on in a shapeless way.

Change your play routines

Get out of the 'every morning I go for a run' mindset. Be a bit of a rebel or perhaps, less threateningly, just an individual who is their own person. Stay in bed late occasionally. Go for a long walk, a really long one. Spend time in the pub with some colleagues.

Stop being so predictable. Surprise yourself.

Walk different routes

Walk where you've never been before, where you have to concentrate. See how many different things you can see. In Donna Leon's novels about Venice, Police Commissario Guido Brunetti rewards himself with a cup of espresso every time he sees something in Venice he hasn't noticed before or a small glass of wine if it's a new and particularly special sight.

Change your form of transport

When did you last go on the top of a bus or travel in a stretch limousine or ride a bicycle or a motorbike or a hot air balloon? Just try seeing things from a different perspective by travelling differently.

Do something out of character

Try selling stuff in the street. Try acting. Try busking. Push yourself into a zone of discomfort. Don't carry this out of control. All we're trying to achieve is give a jolt to your psyche not give you a heart attack.

Get above the detail and start to see more

Elsewhere I've deplored 'wacky stabs in the dark' being passed off as sound creative methodology. I've said that having a properly thought through brief and then paying attention to robust data is required to produce a business solution that is pragmatic and buyable by others.

 **tip**

Condense your argument to a few slides or a simple speech.

But as well as delving deep amongst the trees to recognise that illusive wood we also have to see the wood as a whole. We have to be able to see the big picture, which for most people is really hard. Here are three techniques which will help you think from a helicopter perspective, above the detail.

Mentally walk the 'shop'

This means thinking about what a given business really feels like. Imagine being a camera on the ceiling above it all watching what goes on. Where are the customers, what do they look like, where are the pressure points, what feels hot, what feels cold, what feels right, what jars, what feels as though it has potential and yet is underperforming?

 **tip**

> Imagine you are a satellite looking down on the scene and seeing how all the elements fit together and how people interact.

Have lucid dreams

This is the process whereby you envisage every single detail, smell, sound, sight of a potential experience. Start every other sentence with '**Imagine that**...'. Lucid dreaming allows you to steer your imagination broadly where you want it and generate surprising and previously unthought-of insights.

See things from other viewpoints

How would your mother see the issue you are dealing with? How would you describe it so she could clearly understand it? Do the same assuming it was an eight-year-old child. Do the same assuming it was a journalist versed in your business sector and finally do the same assuming it was a competitor. (Because oddly our competitors are often more astute at seeing our challenges and how they could be solved than we ourselves are.)

 'If there is any one secret of success, it lies in the ability to get the other person's point of view and see things from that person's angle as well as from your own.'

Henry Ford

Exercising eyes, minds and powers of observation

The exercises described above start to make an important difference. They start to inspire curiosity. They awaken thoughts and they change perceptions. Most important of all they move your mind around a problem so you see it from different viewpoints and apply different realities to it. To help take this forward even further, develop some real-life experiences relevant to your own market which will give you anecdotes, new things that you see, new thoughts that you might have, conversations on your journey or anything which sparks off new ideas.

 **tip**

The single biggest aid to creative thinking is to dispel the abstract and get 'down-and-dirty', real, hands-on experience.

Your market

Whatever your specific market is, go to your marketplace and see what's happening. If it's fast-moving branded consumer goods, walk around a couple of supermarkets watching and listening. If it's expensive liquor go to a trendy bar and soak up the atmosphere. If it's banking walk around Canary Wharf and wonder at it all. If it's travel go to World Travel Market Exhibition at Excel to people watch and eavesdrop.

Humans

Whether we are selling ice cream or plastic cans, perfume or photocopiers the human interaction is what counts.

 **tip**

Watch how people respond to other people and to different situations. Learn what makes them 'tick'.

The magic of creativity is that it can, like real magic, capture people's imagination and change the way they think and behave. All creatively minded people in business that I know are pretty good 'people-watchers'. So you be one too. It will help you get ideas and it will make you more observant.

Turn reality on its head

Look at your market or a specific situation within it in very different ways by applying insights from different markets.

Examples of disruptive creative thinking might include:

- What would happen if your product was free?
- What would happen if you had to join a club to get it (like Nespresso)?
- How could you get more people to try your product?
- How could you get your people to work harder?
- Could you simplify the way things work in your business?
- How price sensitive is your product? What could you do to it which would justify a premium price? What would happen if you reduced the price?
- Imagine you were operating in a different market where the rules and processes are completely distinctive – what would change in the way you work?

Magic: think backwards

This is Nick Fitzherbert's[2] idea. It's what magicians do he says. They go to where they want to get to and then track backwards from there, working out in reverse how they got there.

▶ **brilliant** example

Here's a good business outcome: we improved productivity by 25 per cent and reduced waste to insignificant levels. How did we do this?

↓

3rd milestone – all usable waste recycled back into production from previously insignificant levels.

↓

2nd milestone – all production workers were asked to work out how to reduce the number of people working on this process. They came up with a reduction of 4 out of 11 putting those 4 onto the development of a new production line.

↓

1st milestone – we got everyone together to see how to increase productivity of line A – crude reward: a big night out together if we can achieve 20 per cent saving – emphasise 'no one's job at risk'. All these front line workers to sort it out – a bottom-up not top-down solution.

↓

The problem: productivity on line A needs improving and waste needs reducing which if done would produce a big profit improvement.

 **tip**

Visualise the destination first and then plot the journey.

It's also a fact of life that if you think of where you want to get to, your brain and instincts will tend to take you there.

Get bugs out of the system and out of your brain

When you're overrun by e-mails and voice mail what do you do?

Transfer all the e-mails from one PC to another then delete the lot so you can truthfully say: 'I've just transferred all my e-mails to my other PC and lost the lot – if urgent please re-send.' Or change your phone number. Or just wipe the lot pleading insanity or drunkenness or your small child playing with Mummy's computer or sabotage by Henry which you can't explain for legal reasons. Seriously, if only about 10 per cent of all e-mails matter don't ruin your life for 90 per cent of rubbish. Remember Sturgeon's law?

Your team are not helping each other

You don't have to be a great team leader, all you have to do is have a chat over a few beers on the topic of 'how can we work better together?' Try to find out what needs to change to unblock the system. It may be a clash of personalities or confusion over who does what or a bad brief or it might be you… who knows? Well you'd better find out and fix it. Start informally and off the record. Then, if necessary, have a short action meeting. Whatever you do, end up with a simple 'plan-to-fix-it'.

My untidy office drives me crazy

Of course it does but having a good tidy up is very therapeutic. Don't be obsessed about being tidy or untidy… just put it right every so often. But it could be worse.

 'If a cluttered desk is a sign of a cluttered mind, of what, then, is an empty desk a sign?'

'I'm stuck in a rut'

Fix it. Binge on stimuli. Go shopping and use your eyes. Get excited. Also try the following.

Magazines – buy a lot and a box of chocolates to eat as you read them. The *Sun* is read by more people than any other paper. So find out what they're thinking about; you'll be pleasantly surprised. Read the *Week* and get up to date in half an hour – the best news crib ever produced. Read *Private Eye* to realise there are still evangelists for truth around – besides which it's funny. Look at the best of YouTube. Watch a couple of TED talks (they always move me and make me think).

 **tip**

Take your brain on an 'action holiday' – stimulate it with a lot of different and new things. Creativity thrives with surprises.

I feel negative at present

Pouring cold water on any idea is very easy. It's easier to find fault than build on an idea. Negative body language and 'yes but-ism' can even see off genius. So write a list of positive words and try to embed them in the way you think and speak... no not the whole time; don't overdo it... you'll go crazy and others will think you're on drugs. ('Why is he smiling like that? It's creepy.') This is not so much for your benefit (because by now you should be beginning to get the sense of how to unlock your creative potential). No, I'm thinking of the others who will be transformed by your positive responses.

Here are four words that we should all use more **'thank you; well done'**. Let's start by assuming that people are trying to do their best. Let's try and get that best to be even better. It's our job to inspire great creative thinking not to be fixated on just getting to the great creative thought.

Stuck? Jump start the process of creative thinking

You are about to go to a workshop. If you could write a few words on a card to get you through the day they would be these big ten questions:

1 What?

2 Why?

3 How?

4 Where?

5   When?

6   How much?

7   Why not?

8   What if?

9   Where next?

10 What next?

Notes

1   Lao Tsu dates back to, possibly, the 6th century BC. He is an ancient Chinese philosopher and central figure in Taoism but he is also revered as a deity in religious Taoism and traditional Chinese religions.

2   Nick Fitzherbert was in PR for 20 years and ran his own PR agency. He's a member of the Magic Circle and applies the rules of magic to presenting and creative thinking. His book *Presentation Magic* is an important contribution.

CHAPTER 12

Creating brilliant creative-thinking workshops

Preparing for group work

Give yourself and your co-creative spirits the best chance of making a 'creative workshop' work brilliantly.

Who are you?

Virtually everyone has to introduce themselves at meetings or workshops. They usually do it rather badly and very apologetically.

'Hi, I'm Richard. I sort of work in procurement which is, well, quite interesting and I want to see how today goes really… and I suppose that's about it really.'

Practise so you have an introduction that has more impact and which tries to be a bit different and a bit creative.

'The chairs you're sitting on, the light bulbs above our heads, the daffodil bulbs in the gardens are here because of me because I'm a buyer. I'm in procurement. My name is Richard. And today I guess I'll be buying into creativity.'

That's better… a bit more interesting at any rate. Nothing beats trying to be interesting.

'Team techniques' for creative workshops

This is the time to try a few group techniques in creative thinking and see just how creative you all can really be. And the chances are that you'll be surprised that not only can you swim but that you can also do butterfly, crawl and backstroke.

 **tip**

The more creative exercises you do the more creative you'll get and the more you do, the more you'll want to do.

This chapter is the handbook for the techniques that make workshops fly and there are enough techniques here to enable you to make the first few workshops all interestingly different from each other. But, a word of warning: warm-up exercises are not nice-to-haves. They are essential. We're dealing with complex and precious equipment here – your brains – so treat them with respect.

Secondly, most of what you'll be doing in these workshops will be what is just second nature to a seven-year-old child. There's nothing here that in the deeper recesses of your unconscious won't have the neurons chattering away 'been there, done that'. Creative workshops, when done well, are enormously productive and even better fun. Take your time. Be patient. Start the engine. And whenever you are ready, put your foot down... .

Why do a workshop?

This is the most important question you can ask. If you don't have a clear set of objectives or understand that the issue you need to fix is just one minor thing then you oughtn't to be running a workshop at all. Be clear with all your delegates before they arrive as to what the real aim of the day is.

 **tip**

Workshops should have big objectives and be treated seriously.

Who's it for?

Do not try and run a productive day with more than 10 people. When you have a roomful of 12 or more you are a hostage to mob rule. But if you need to accommodate more people, there is of course a simple solution which is to run two workshops.

It's strange that some people don't seem to think the numbers matter. They do. With 10 (or better still eight) you can create and control momentum.

Do not invite anyone to attend who is a dyed-in-the-wool cynic or has no real need to be there or any contribution to make.

Where do you hold it?

Always try and do it off-site with all mobiles off (or better still persuade people to leave their mobiles at the office). For preference, try to find somewhere interesting with a decent view. Try to avoid windowless or underground rooms. And if the budget stretches to it, try and stay overnight. This secures a fast start in the morning provided people don't stay up very late drinking too much which nowadays is much less likely than it used to be.

If it has to be in the office make sure that the room is dressed up a little so it looks as though the person organising this 'event' cares about it. Whatever else ensure that you avoid making it look like 'business as usual' because it isn't.

A workshop is '**business as unusual**'.

What's the format; what will happen?

Remember to use the word **'event'**.

If the day is really going to be a success make sure it's a memorable day so people talk about **'the event'** afterwards.

The four things that really matter are:

- **Good facilitation** or chairing of the event. The motive is to keep everything moving at a good, business-like pace. It means involving everyone. And it needs a person leading it who, when necessary, can inspire people to think not just chair the meeting.

- **A clear and thorough briefing** on what is going to happen. If you have seven hours available try to break the day into say no more than five segments. Make sure there is enough time at the end to drive towards a conclusion.

- **Branding and art direction** of the room and all the material used is really important as this is what sticks in people's minds and the event is given a particular style, focus and sense of importance.

- **A brief and interesting record** of the day... 'brief' is harder than expansive by the way. It's good to make it semi-visual with photographs of people at work. You might also include some great quotes on creativity in it so other people seeing it get a sense it was serious and get a sense of the key substance of the day.

There are a lot of well used and effective tools from which you can choose. In general if you have just a day to solve a problem there are a few things to bear in mind.

 **tip**

Make sure everyone arrives ready to 'go'. Start the day with everyone on the same page and 'warmed up'. People should be ready to go for it and get stuck in.

Throughout the day try to get broad alignment but don't aim for blind obedience.

You should only expect to use at most three techniques, bearing in mind these are tools to help everyone maximise their creative thinking. None of them are magical; all of them are pragmatic ways of helping people think more adventurously.

A few rules

- No invalidation of ideas – no cynical challenge and pushback.
- We need a lot of ideas, not just a few good ones.
- Big, colourful and off-the-wall ideas are helpful.
- We need to 'build' on ideas and see how to improve them.
- Everyone is equal – this is not a hierarchical game.

Power creativity tools

These are well used and work well – provided the chair/facilitator of the event drives things along energetically and at speed and maintains everyone's good spirits.

 tip

Ensure *everyone* has their say. Avoid the danger of the noisiest person dominating.

Brainstorms (or 'thought showers' as some prefer to call them)

Alex Osborn, an advertising man, created the idea of brainstorming in 1941 claiming that the technique increased idea generation by 44 per cent (which sounds suspiciously like ad man statistics to me). It is quite simply a free-thinking, generative process where nothing is taken for granted and where the association and connection of ideas is encouraged. Having encouraging, highly participative chairing will make brainstorms exhausting but productive and fun.

No one owns an idea in a brainstorm but the idea is to get everyone to blurt out ideas. Make these sessions move at great speed with lots of encouragement to participants.

Comment

Current thinking is that brainstorming, which was originally used best as a teaching technique, is a bit childish and favours the superficial. The absence of focus and critical thinking can be an impediment to useful innovation, some suggest. The counter argument is it jump starts creative thinking and removes inhibition. That alone makes it valuable.

Lateral thinking

Edward de Bono's concept of 'lateral thinking' is out on its own as a technique for more sophisticated users. It's 'brainstorming' but with a bit more focus.

First of all agree the task, the terms of reference, the format and outcomes you want:

- Clearly set up the task, the objectives and the background.
- Constantly break up the way of working and thinking so no one settles into a rut.

Then get people to think in different ways by asking them to imagine, challenge and think:

- Imagine you could have anything you wanted to solve this problem – what would it be?
- Think opposites (what's the opposite of what you have? How could you make your processes work really badly?)
- Think similarities (what else is this like?)

- Make people challenge facts (must your situation always be like this? Imagine removing all obstacles to change).
- Encourage people to change all the rules.
- What if? Why not? Encourage different thoughts. Encourage creativity.

Finally, capture ideas because they're precious and hard fought for and capturing them shows respect for the team's output:

- Write stuff down so ideas get recorded – A2 pads, lots of magic marker colours. Legibility matters so get people to write clearly.
- Stick the sheets on the walls.
- Make sure the best ideas are agreed on by most people.

Comment

If you like 'brainstorming' this makes it a little more sophisticated and it gives the facilitator a few more levers to pull. It's sort of 'brainstorming 2' if you like. Brainstorming with more structured challenges.

 **tip**

Three hours of intensive, open debate and group thinking is about as much as any group can take on one topic.

Thought-building

It's the same concept as 'brainstorming' to start with but conducted by e-mail rather than in person. It then develops into the game of *Consequences* where half-formed ideas are built on in e-mails and passed on and passed on again to people in the original 'brainstorming group' to refine and build on. This works especially well with a group of smart people trying to crack a very hard problem. 'Thought-building' is also a great way of keeping the energy of a productive group from a workshop alive after the 'workshop' is over.

Comment

This is a powerful way of sharing ideas and building on them quickly over a day or two. It requires cryptic comments if it's to work at its best. This is a useful way of mounting a fast, thoughtful discussion with people in far-flung locations all over the world.

Scenario building

Michael Porter[1] said this was where he really saw the value of creativity in forming strategy. Because, he suggested, you cannot solve problems in isolation of the context in which they exist.

A simple example of this would be 'how do we increase sales?' which means different things in a recession and in a growth market. Speculating what the future might look like and illustrating it with specifics can be very stimulating and useful.

 **tip**

Scenario building is a brilliant way of getting a group to exercise their creative muscles and learn the art of storytelling.

Here are some ideas to start with on which a workshop can creatively chew:

- It's 2020… what's the world looking like seen through the eyes of the man or woman in the street?
- Who's the US President? What happened?
- Who's in power in the UK? What twists and turns led to this?
- What are the leading cars, beers, restaurants, retailers, foods, fashions, types of music, holiday destinations etc.?

- What's the weather like?
- What are the key items in the news?
- What does our own market look and feel like – what's changed?

Comment

Scenario planning is the most effective way of wrenching busy executives away from their day-to-day issue and processes. It forces people to address the issue of change by making change real. Because it's a work of fiction it unleashes great waves of creative thinking.

Mind-mapping

This is a powerful way of creating order out of chaos and teasing out the vast body of knowledge, perception of patterns and connections a group of motivated people can generate. The technique proves how much we know when we create the right structures even if we didn't know we knew all that before we started. It's a powerful way of starting a workshop of yet-to-be-convinced delegates.

► brilliant **example**

How many types of tree, uses of trees, fruit from trees etc. can a group come up with, in half an hour, without mind-mapping and then with mind-mapping? Break into two groups and see.

Here's how it works

A 'mind map' is a diagram used to visually outline information. It's often created around a single word or text, placed in the centre, to which associated ideas, words and concepts are added. Major categories radiate from a central node, and lesser categories are sub-branches of larger branches. Categories can represent words, ideas, tasks or other items related to a central key word. Mind maps can be drawn by hand, either as 'rough notes' during a lecture or meeting, for example, or as higher quality pictures when more time is available. Mind maps are a type of spider diagram.

Comment

Sherlock Holmes and his 'mind palace' will have made anyone familiar with that TV series aware of this concept. It's a memory technique whereby you track back in your memory to retrieve facts. Its power lies in structured word and concept association forcing collective memories to open and possibly fruitful connections to be made.

 **tip**

You never actually forget things. You just need to find them in your mind.

Word association

This is like mind-mapping without the structure and can very simply be best regarded as a 'mind-loosener' which helps people get in the swing of a free association creative-thinking session.

It works best when done in sequence going round a group. If you can't think of a word say 'pass'. Interesting to do this first at the beginning and then, again, at the end of a session to prove how dramatically everyone's improved..

▶ **brilliant example**

Loss – funeral – closure – recuperation – renewal – birth – growth – city – noise – excitement – bars – people – laughter – opportunity – friends – sharing – shares – sell – cash-in – re-invest....

Comment

It's good fun as a game and as a mental lubricant. But don't expect to get any lasting value from it.

Focusing on specific features

The power of detail is important in helping develop ideas but not just detail, but detail which translates into human benefits. Doug Hall[2] (no relation) in his book *Jump Start Your Business Brain* develops the sales argument for Armor Shoe Polish engagingly thus:

Basic feature: human benefit

Fast shoeshine: 2 minute shine
Durable shine: 7 day shine
Protects shoes: Salt guard v. winter damage
For all shoes: Gentle shine for delicate shoes
Whole shoe care: Special anti-slip for soles

What you should learn from this is what any advertising copywriter will learn on day one in a decent advertising agency – be specific. Make a benefit a tangible fact not a generalised claim. Learning how to describe a situation or a product in the kind of detail that involves and excites people can be transformational in helping create a really exciting workshop especially in the generation of new product ideas.

 **tip**

Facts are sexy.

Comment

Very worthwhile when examining a specific product or service. It will only work if you can manage to do it as shown. First assemble the basic features then, after a break, drill down and develop these to become 'what's-specifically-in-it-for-the-con-sumer' benefits.

Creating a group creative thinking environment

Creativity without constant nourishment for the brain via stimuli won't work very well. In today's fast-moving, unforgiving, nose-to-the-grindstone world there seems so little time for many business people to watch films or read magazines, let alone books, in a relaxed way. But it has to be done if you are to reach maestro creative-thinking status.

The 'long walk'

This is a brilliant way of starting a 'workshop'. All of the group split into two teams and go for a long walk down a high street and through a shopping centre the afternoon before the creative day or on the morning of the day itself. Using their mobile phones to take pictures they then, at the workshop itself, identify 10 big trends in retail or society that are going to inform their view of the future. The big story could be anything or anyone from a Big Issue salesman playing the fool, a child stroking a cat, an overflowing litterbin or a new branch of W.H. Smith.

 **tip**

> The first trick is to be on the look-out for the unusual. The second trick is to relax in each other's company.

Thinking in colour

We live in a technicolour world in which we keep using monochrome minds. It's the nature of work today that we lose our sense of virtually everything except for the task in hand and survival. This game involves our using pastels – messy but easier to clean than paint – working as a team and constructing a mural on lots of A2 sheets pinned together of a subject like 'The High Street of the Future', 'The Office of the Future', 'The Seaside of the Future', 'The Motorway of the Future'. It helps to have a semi-professional artist on site to draw the outlines under instruction. The participants' role is to colour in what the artist has given them.

Colour speaks. Try it. This requires lots of boldness and expressiveness. I don't recommend spending too long on this or doing it with people who aren't workshop attuned. To those who are it's a source of potential mind lubrication.

Reducing a story to pictures

If it is true that 'a picture is worth a thousand words' then we should spend more time building our corporate picture libraries. Whenever you see a good picture – one that describes what you do or feel, capture it because thinking visually and not just in documents is an intensely liberating experience.

 **tip**

Google images allow a limitless source of material to build a pictorial story which will evoke more response than words alone can usually do.

Using our senses – touch, taste, smell, hearing, sight

I am suspicious of mood-boards which are at best very approximate things and often totally misleading. Whenever I see them I am reminded that advertising professionals simply do a great job and how very good art directors really are. A 'mood room', however, which touches every sense is a better place in which to hold a 'workshop' about a business issue that needs resolving. How for instance would you create the mood room for the House of Commons?

Primary/secondary

- **Touch:** lots of paper; leather chairs
- **Smell:** dust and whisky; old changing rooms
- **Sight:** barristers' wigs; cornices and crumpled suits
- **Taste:** school food; Fisherman's Friends
- **Sound:** sheep baah-ing; men snoring

Seeing things from different perspectives

Reversal

I just love this one and think everyone should use it daily. Ask the opposite of what you want, for instance, 'how could we sell a lot less of this than we currently do?' or 'how could we worsen our customer satisfaction?' or 'what small change would make our product much worse?' In the answers, small but very telling truths can emerge like 'do more of what we currently do – that should make things worse'. This might force you to examine whether the seeds for the brand's destruction don't already exist. GE created an exercise during the dot.com boom which was designed to test how vulnerable it was. Executives had to work out what would bring down the division in which they worked. It was called 'destroyyourowncompany.com'.

Distortion

Make the dimensions of the issue you are dealing with either much smaller or much larger. For example:

- Suppose the problem we are talking about existed only in just one town like Bath – how would we address it?
- Suppose this was a global problem and getting worse. How would we deal with this commercial pandemic?
- Suppose this was the only problem you had… what would you do?

 **tip**

Break a problem down into small chunks. Change the size, shape and context too. Rough the problem up a bit. I call this 'creative mugging'.

Identification

I think this concept is brilliant. Chris Dugdale[3] (a magician like Nick Fitzberbert) has a three-part creative solution to most problems which relies on empathy, identification and resolution. Try saying this to anyone who comes to you with a problem and see how well it works:

'I know how you feel about (whatever)… I felt the same way when (whatever happened to me)… but I found that when I did (whatever)… everything worked out just fine.'

Dislocation

I heard this one (more or less in this form) from ex advertising man, Len Weinreich. There are, he said, six glasses of clear liquid in front of you. Examine the different ways with which you respond to each of them as I tell you that they are respectively:

- tap water
- bleach
- pure spring water from 'Ochran Mill' in the Wye Valley
- sulphuric acid
- saki
- vodka.

Playing the game like this – in which nothing is quite as it at first seems – is a potent way of creating new product concepts. Hence Croft Original which looked sophisticatedly pale but had the sweet hit of Harvey's Bristol Cream. Having a deceptive appearance is the root of Heston Blumenthal's formula. It reminds us never to take anything at face value. But its real value in terms of creative thinking is to see whether you can transfer the 'looks weak/tastes strong: looks sweet/tastes bitter' idea to other markets or situations where you want to shake up people's thinking.

 **tip**

> Never take anything at face value. The ultimate in creative thinking is to imagine that anything is possible.

Using fresh eyes

Get people to imagine they'd just won a large sum of money and that they've bought the business in which they currently work. As the 100 per cent shareholder they have carte blanche to do what they want with it. It's their money; their choice; their business.

- What three big things would they change?
- What products would they drop?
- Where would they locate head office?
- Would they want a big head office at all?
- How would they change the marketing?
- Where would they reduce focus and resources?
- Where would they increase focus and resources?
- Who would they recruit?

What would they expect the company to look like in three years' time? This is best used at the end of a session when people feel relaxed, honest and courageous. It's also probably best kept 'off the record'.

Sorting out new ideas

Thinking hats revised

Edward de Bono had six thinking hats in his famous book called *Six Thinking Hats* which I just think is too many hats. Here's what the colours stood for:

- **White** – about information.
- **Red** – about emotions and feelings.
- **Black** – about caution, criticism and challenge.
- **Yellow** – about optimism and positive thoughts.
- **Green** – about creativity and opportunities.
- **Blue** – about seeing things from above – deep thought.

I'd prefer just three. (**Red** – how do you feel about the opportunities? What is there to get excited and emotional about? **Green** – about creativity and opportunities. **Black** – what should we worry about?) I'd also prefer them as T-shirts which are more comfortable to wear on a long away-day. They are also harder to take off and discard than hats so you're stuck with them.

The T-shirt wearers can generate ideas in their respective thinking modes. But at the end of the day as a team they can go through a sieving process of the day's work. From their different perspectives they can sort out the weaknesses and strengths of different ideas. This can provide a pretty sophisticated check.

Good, bad and interesting ideas

Research, according to De Bono, has shown that when people are asked to sort ideas into 'good, bad and interesting' usually the most useful ideas (or half-formed ideas or ideas that might lead to other ideas) sit in the 'interesting' category not in the 'good' category. Try this yourself at the end of a workshop so the half-formed 'interesting' gems aren't lost.

 **tip**

> It's adolescent ideas rather than fully formed concepts that are often the acorns that have got the biggest promise.

Brand new ideas need to be seized and developed

New ideas need to be grabbed and wrestled to the ground as one pundit said, just creep up on them when they aren't looking, seize them and make them your own.

Storytelling

Make everyone around you become a good storyteller. It's a skill everyone in business needs. But first you need a structure:

A beginning:

- Introducing the issue
- Introducing the characters
- Introducing the problem

A middle:

- What the characters do to investigate the problem
- How big a problem this really is
- What the options are for resolving it – a dramatic debate

An end:

- The solutions are interrogated to see which of them seems to work best
- They are subjected to many tests
- Dramatically the winner emerges after several tussles

The word 'narrative' is one increasingly used by business leaders. The role of stories in business helps everyone distil their thinking into a memorable format.

Agenda-less conversation

This may not always be practical! What If? (the marketing company) recommends taking a cottage on a moor for a few days and having a conversation about the issue without a specific agenda. Whilst I love the focus and the mood of 'no one leaves here till we get this sorted', I somehow doubt if many people would do it. Perhaps they should.

Perhaps more practical is Lawrie Philpott's[4] concept of the long country walk from a country station. Meet there and plan a five-mile hike. No notes and no agenda, just a long rambling conversation over two hours during which the big stuff always comes out (those lurking elephants come lumbering into plain sight he finds). It concludes with a country pub lunch. Bring walking shoes and an open mind. Underlying the concept is that there is enough time to dig really deep into describing a problem, listening to various ideas, generating new ones and talking about how to solve a problem.

 **tip**

Half the joy is being free of the office, mobile and pressures of the job. The other half is discovering the hidden creative thinker in all of us.

Emptying your brains of preconceptions

I've talked about the disabling impact 'misleading prejudgements' have. It's difficult to switch off our subconscious 'pre-conceiver' but if we realise it's switched on we can constantly neutralise it by thinking:

'*No I have not yet made up my mind about anything. I'm still in listening mode.*'

In order to have a clear mind and the opportunity to think new thoughts it's important that the pre-conceiver is on 'idle' because it's this pre-conceiver which is likely to stop you listening and finding new solutions to the problem you have.

 **tip**

Switch off your pre-conceiver. Switch on your receiver.

Mind-dumping

This is 'brainstorming' without any rules. It's an agenda-less hour simply allowing your team to get everything and anything off their chests and out of their brains; saying all the things that come into your collective heads as a group.

 **tip**

Allow your team the forum to tell you anything that's annoying them or anything which seems to be a good idea.

It will prove as therapeutic to get rid of a lot of mental rubbish as it is to tidy your office. It also motivates everyone if it becomes reasonably regular, allowing everyone to 'unload' bad stuff as well as good ideas.

 **recap**

Broadly there are three typical situations:

- **A business problem** or group of problems that need sorting. (Example: the factory in Lille is, in terms of productivity, below other factories in the group.)
- **A big strategic issue.** (Example: where is this business going? where could it go? what does it take to get it there?)
- **Innovation.** The need to create new products to refresh the current portfolio.

Five brilliant steps to unleashing group creativity

Old lady: 'How do I get to Carnegie Hall, Officer?'

Policeman: 'Practise, lady, practise.'

Brilliant step one: practising

Have the curiosity and confidence to focus on half a dozen of the techniques described and practise them. Practise them until they become second nature.

Choose the ones that suit *you* and which you most enjoy. Here are mine:

- **The long walk** – window shopping and people watching. Trying to work out what is going on out there in the real world.
- **Mind-mapping** – this is a brilliant way of unearthing all those things in the grey to dark, half-forgotten area of your memory.
- **Reversal** – doing what would achieve the exact opposite of what you want can sometimes expose exactly what it is you are now doing that is wrong.

- **Thinking backwards** – allows you to define and actually picture success and plot how it was you got there step by step. It's a kind of 'pre-rationalisation' and one of the most creative tools there is.

- **The stimuli binge** – here's how: sitting down with a pile of books, papers, magazines, spending an hour surfing the net, listening to Radio Four, spending a couple of hours flicking through the different TV channels. And they call this work... but it is... creative work.

Brilliant step two: perfect conditions

- **When's** your best time of day? Morning or evening. Are you a lark or an owl?

- **Where** do you feel most relaxed when working? Think about **where** you feel most productive.

- Do you prefer thinking onto a PC, a laptop or onto an A4 or A2 pad?

- Do you prefer silence or background music?

- Do you have enough light? Research shows we perform much better in bright light.

- Do you want it warmer or cooler?

- What's your ideal mood in which to be?

- Do you want it tidy or untidy? A large number of people I've spoken to go on a tidying up frenzy before they start work. Others like unstructured chaos.

 **tip**

When you feel just right then it's time to start. Do not take off before you've gone through your 'creative pre-flight check'.

Brilliant step three: simmer.

I have talked about dreaming as a way of achieving creativity. The other way is to ensure that the key ingredients of the issue you are trying to solve are given the space and time to stew in your brain without you trying to come to any particular conclusion. Not coming to a conclusion is hard because we've been educated to look at an equation or a question and answer it before that invigilator says 'will you stop writing now?' The process I'm describing lets the intuitive part of our brain take the issue and then gently cook it.

I love the idea of stewing ideas in the Aga of your mind.

Brilliant step four: 'I remember...'

Recall an occasion when you had a lot of good thoughts. Recall the place and the situation.

What was it that made this stand out? What was special? What was different? Remember when everything felt great for you and you came up effortlessly with great ideas. Just recalling that will help you reconnect with your creative inner self.

Brilliant step five: self-confidence

Whenever you are asked to come up with some creative ideas there is a sequence of thinking that helps get you running on that creative treadmill. Say these words to yourself:

- I can do this.
- I shall do it very well.
- I am the master or mistress of my own thinking.
- I shall discard more ideas than I keep.
- This will be fun.

Workshops can be wonderful or woeful
We've all experienced group stupidity, when a group discussion

concludes a series of things that make one scratch one's head in bewilderment. Usually this is because the group has tribal links of some kind. We can imagine a group of Chelsea football fans or a group of investment bankers both coming up with a bunch of strange and introspectively self-serving ideas.

However, most reasonably diverse groups of people demonstrate three tendencies:

- A likelihood that they will be accurate in their collective judgements.
- A probability that they will have a sense of collective responsibility. People are, in the main, fair minded and unselfish.
- An astonishing ability, once prompted, to have creative ideas.

To make these happen everyone has to feel their views are valued. The occasion on which their creativity is being sought needs to feel like an event worth attending. The rules of engagement need to be clear and the facilitation needs to be inspiring, energetic and positive.

There needs to be some patience as well. It sometimes takes time for the barriers of scepticism to be dismantled and people get a bit tired especially after lunch. Better to start early and work through, with snacking on the hoof, to finish early. There are no rules that say creativity works 9.00–5.00.

 **recap**

No one can be creative all the time any more than they can be always cheerful. Creativity is best attempted when you are feeling relaxed. Having said which, I am no fan of being precious about searching for, thinking around or writing about new ideas. You have to start sometime so 'now' is always as good as any other time. Creative thinking in business starts with that brief. If you have that brief even what can seem, at the time, like abortive fumbles at creatively answering it are in fact the first steps to solving it, even if you subsequently discard them. Creativity is a constant state of mind not a magical tap that you turn on and off. It's dripping away all the time. So just gather the drops and see what happens.

Notes

1   Michael Porter is, to many, the God of business strategy. He was born in 1947 and is Professor at The Institute for Strategy and Competitiveness, based at Harvard Business School. He is the leading authority on competitive strategy and competitiveness. His 'five competitive forces' is an important contribution to management thinking. These are, he says: existing competitive rivalry between suppliers; threat of new market entrants; bargaining power of buyers; power of supplier; threat of substitute products (including technology change). He's written 18 books. Professor Porter is the most cited author in business and economics.

2   Doug Hall is an American inventor, author and entrepreneur. He is a chemical engineer by education who rose to become Master Marketing Inventor at Procter & Gamble. He is the Founder and CEO of the Eureka! Ranch. Doug is another of a long line of innovation evangelists.

3   As an award winning close-up magician Chris Dugdale is unparalleled. He is the only magician in history to have been selected to entertain the Queen and the United Nations.

4   Lawrie Philpott is the founder of Philpott Black, a consultancy specialising in leadership, change management and top team challenges. He was previously a partner for 17 years at Coopers and Lybrand.

PART 6

Thinking of other people

You cannot lead people if you don't listen to them. You cannot lead people if you don't put yourself in their position. The most important skill is to be seen to understand them well enough so they follow you willingly. You'll do this by inspiring them, involving them and thinking about how they think. Don't just tell them to do something. Get on their wavelength. This is called 'altrocentric leadership' ('altrocentric' is the opposite of egocentric) and leaders of today are expected to be good at it... or else.

CHAPTER 13

How to get on other people's wavelengths

The big word of today is 'empathy'. A few years ago a manager wouldn't have known what it meant but now it's as hot in management as social media is in marketing. Can't empathise = can't manage = unemployable. So put your people-thinking hat on fast.

Any business where there isn't a high level of trust throughout the team is in trouble. As Elvis Presley sang:

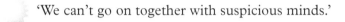

'We can't go on together with suspicious minds.'

Unless we can build relationships based on trust, our working lives will be difficult. Christopher Locke in *The Cluetrain Manifesto* describes a vision of the future that most of us would sign up to:

'Imagine a world where everyone was constantly learning, a world where what you wondered was more interesting than what you knew and curiosity counted for more than certain knowledge.'

Yes. I'd sign up to that. And also to a world where people forgave each other.

Rodney King was famously beaten up by the LA Police after a high speed car chase in 1991. King had criminal form and was not a blameless individual but his words are noble:

'Please can we all get along ... I mean we're stuck here for a while... we can sort it out.'

Empathy is what we all need more of

In its simplest form, empathy is what it is to feel like being in someone else's shoes. We can get empathy through reading a novel or seeing a play. We can 'feel' the pain, the rage or the desire and it's probably impossible for us to torture people if we can empathise with them. And it seems to be unique to humans since even the most developed primates appear not to empathise.

Looking very briefly at the science, neuroscientists like Marco Iacoboni[1] have argued that mirror neuron systems in the human brain help us understand the actions and intentions of other people by quite simply mirroring what other people do. He argues that mirror neurons are the neural basis of the human capacity for empathy which is the very key to our understanding the actions of other people.

In the business world the importance of this is self-evident.

brilliant tip

Understanding others is a business essential. Unless you can think like others you can't succeed at marketing, management, innovation or anything.

Without empathy, marketing and sales are very tricky and without empathy managing a team of people is, at the very least, problematic. To help him in his job Ian Parker, CEO of Red Star Equity, runs low-intensity psychometric tests to avoid what he calls unnecessary 'misunderstanding'. Which makes sense but you can only understand others if you understand yourself.

Here's how Alexander Solzhenitsyn put it:

'If you want to change the world who do you begin with – yourself or others? I believe if we begin with ourselves and do the things we

need to do and become the best person we can be we must have a
better chance of changing the world for the better.'

The more we study this subject of people and their behaviour
and ourselves and our own behaviour, the more we realise we
aren't irrational we're just rather inconsistent. For instance, we
might speculate quite dramatically about how someone potentially might behave towards us and we might get cross about
their hypothetical potential unreasonableness and end up having
a fight in our minds with them: 'I'll never speak to him again.
Bastard!!'

But hang on… you've just made this all up. Get back to reality.
Step into his shoes. Assume good nature might prevail… what
then?

Sam Richards[2] is a brilliant speaker as well as being an academic. His 'radical experiment in empathy' asks his American
audience to imagine how they'd feel if the Chinese invaded
the USA on a 'peacekeeping mission' but with the generally
understood motive of protecting their coal interests. And then
switches to making the audience empathise with the Iraqis – yes
even the terrorists. It's compelling. It also shows empathy isn't
always comfortable. Sam asks us to 'swap one tiny world for
another tiny world' and quotes Dostoyevsky: 'Nothing is easier
than to denounce the evil doer; nothing is more difficult than to
understand him.' If this doesn't help you want to learn how to
empathise then nothing will.

Unlike other psychological areas like creativity, empathy is an
area of psychology that is being widely and excitingly explored.
An example is the remarkable Brené Brown[3] who's an academic
exploring how people connect with each other. She suggests
we're neurobiologically programmed for human connection and
identifies that in this quest for authentic connection people really
learn to empathise. Essential to it, though, is an acceptance that
life is a bit messy (she confesses, as someone who likes order,

she herself finds this disconcerting) and that admitting to and accepting our own vulnerability is essential to good connecting.

If you think about that it flies in the face of years of alpha males practising 'don't show fear' and Harvard Business School and others teaching the necessity of displaying confidence. Brené says that in her studies what matters most is not people asking 'what's in it for me?' but the increasing cohort asking a much more important question: 'what's in it for *us*?' If she's right, and I think she is, the implication of this for management is significant.

 **tip**

> More people are asking 'what's in it for people like us?' not 'what's in it for me?' This means we've got to think more about groups not individuals.

The concept of community through 'street parties' and 'book clubs' tells us a lot about today's social world. The popularity of LinkedIn and the increasing number of business community groups like the Institute of Directors and Royal Society of Arts tell us a lot about business.

It's the group not the individual who's winning the climb up that greasy pole now.

Finding out more about people

Let's get back to Solzhenitsyn and self-knowledge. In common with most people my own self-knowledge is scantier than I'd thought it was. Until I started studying some basic psychology to help me write this book I thought I was fine but now I'm not so sure. What follows is less than exhaustive (that would be a book in itself) but it briefly highlights some areas to consider in empathising with the people you work with. The key (as with everything in this book) is to ask these two questions: 'what do I think?' and 'what do they think?'

We're human

We'll learn more about them as work colleagues if we first consider them as humans. Rachel Bell's view in interviewing potential candidates is you need a 360° view of their family background. I always spent time looking at hobbies and interests. If it said 'I have none… I live for my work' I was very worried. And it was Daniel Kahneman who proved in research that a better insight into a person was generated by visiting a person's flat than in studying their CV (even when expert HR people were doing the studying). Because we need to know what drives people. What do they do with their lives when they are not working? Do we really understand what makes them tick?

We don't listen

Deborah Tannen[4] has written many books including *You just don't understand* and *That's not what I meant*. Books like these help us understand the problem. Just consider how often a simple e-mail is read different ways by different people. Never assume you've been clear. Ask people to play back what they think you've said.

 **tip**

What matters is what *they* think you said, not what *you* think you said.

We're not all the same

There are lots of different types of people. Harold Leavitt[5] identified three: visionaries, analysts and implementers. In his time (rather a long time ago) he was himself, no doubt, a visionary but

I rather doubt if he practised empathy. Since Harold the world of psychology and management has moved on, as Deborah Tannen points out:

'We all know we are unique individuals, but we tend to see others as representatives of groups.'

Games at work

The community of work encourages alliances, politics and games. The system of incentives in some sectors even encourages 'mild cheating'. The encouragement to win in what's painted as a zero-sum game, where there are fewer winners than actual players in the game, encourages this kind of comment: 'You don't have to read a proposal to demolish it.' Teresa Arbuckle, Chief Marketing Officer at Beko (the market leader in white goods), who's very experienced in the big corporate world noted that this is a results focused/gratification society – awards, market share, bonuses, account wins etc. But she adds there's an irony which is this, getting what you really, really want doesn't necessarily gratify you.

 **tip**

Winning the game and getting what you wanted seldom gratifies you as you thought it would.

Deep down we're nice

Psychological research is ambivalent about this, at best, with various experiments showing the reverse. Allow people to play-act prison warders or torturers and they behave like monsters. In one research experiment respondents were in separate booths and one of them (a plant) simulated having a heart attack. Only a few went to his aid, those who didn't do so apparently assumed that someone else would do so or, seeming indifferent to his fate, just ignored him. In fact Daniel Kahneman says the behaviour of respondents in such situations is generally disappointing. I suspect this is more to do with the play-acting that research environments seem to inspire rather than a reliable indication of people's real feelings. Caveat: don't have a heart attack in a research experiment.

 **tip**

> Real empathy unlocks real instincts by demonstrating understanding.

People hate losing stuff

Research shows we are programmed to dislike losing things we already have. But it goes deeper than material possessions. At a personal level we all seem to want to enrich our store of memories. In a business environment the corporate memory and store of stories is really important in creating a meaningful culture. Here's what Brené Brown says: 'Stories are data with a soul.' That's exactly what they are in business – where spreadsheets and anecdotes meet. Remember that people's thinking starts in their memory and the past. That's the real reference point. So to empathise we need to know of what other people's memory store comprises.

What price loyalty?

A very well paid CEO asked me this question. It belongs to the paternalistic past when Quaker firms like Cadbury, Rowntree and Clark's set up businesses which looked after their employees' education and their physical, moral and cultural welfare. There's a communal and tribal instinct people still have about their 'team' but it's less firmly embedded now than then. It's driven by our wanting to get on together rather than by some anthem or mission statement. If we can understand our colleagues in these terms, their loyalty to us and to our business, our chances of managing and fruitfully working with them are hugely enhanced.

 **tip**

> Don't ask for blind loyalty. Ask for understanding and respect. They are much more valuable.

Avoid overconfidence

Maria Konnikova describes overconfidence as the Achilles heel of any thinker. Think about some of the teams in investment banks in the 2008 banking crisis. The toxic overconfidence we saw from them led to a sense of invulnerability and incaution. It can spring from a long run of success, apparent over familiarity with a business situation leading to taking things for granted, from having so much information that one feels briefed to the point of one's story being watertight or from being so close to the action that one feels in total command.

 **tip**

> Remember that overconfidence is the enemy of learning. In a learning environment empathy thrives because there's a sense of mutual experience.

People are impressionable

In his book *The Righteous Mind* Jonathan Haidt shows how people respond to others' good looks – sorry that doesn't sound very PC but good-looking people on trial (he tells us) are less likely to be found guilty or, if found guilty, will tend to get shorter sentences. The way we respond to anything can be influenced by where we are asked questions, how the room where we're asked smells, what the weather's like or the way we're asked (so much for a lot of research findings). We also like to be seen to conform (most of us). But being able to override this is a mighty help in building substantial relationships. Yes, we like connecting with people and few of us are loners. But if, with a degree of self-amusement, we recognise how impressionable we can all be, we can share this with our colleagues and show we are vulnerable too.

 **tip**

> Don't take yourself too seriously. If we show we too are humanly vulnerable we'll find it easier to connect with others.

We get intimidated very easily

We are so intimidated by experts that we often stop bothering to think at all when they're talking on the basis that they know best. The best coping strategies with smart peers is to recognise their strengths, the ones that we can't match, and to add our own to the mix because the older you get the more you discover everyone has something good to offer.

brilliant tip

> The art of empathy is recognising what the best of everyone is, drawing it out from all of them and then aggregating it.

Looking at things from different points of view

Professor Marcus Alexander says that we're bad at shifting perspectives from planning to logistics to creativity to strategy; actually just bad at shifting perspective, period. 'We see things not as others are but as we are,' said novelist Anaïs Nin. So much, then, for the concept of 'altrocentricity'.

Both views express the great difficulty we have in being empathetic. It does not come as second nature to most of us. Yet only when we get away from our own ego can we see new solutions and other ways of looking at things. It's as though we have a big bully in our head triumphantly shouting the title of the Edward de Bono book: *I am right and you are wrong.*

We all know that team management is the key to change management, that in increasingly complex situations we can't do it all, that delegation and a great team effort is what always makes the difference. Yet nothing changes for many of us. We have meetings, we push stuff through but we're pressed and stressed and in real-time we don't have feedback on what people really feel and actually think.

> Empathy comes at a price. It means letting go of your own ego and it takes time. Things are easier to understand than people and people want more of your time.

Even when we think that we are certain about what needs to be done we should still ask how others see the situation. This is not to denigrate our own judgement as although the way we see things is important there is seldom just a single truth. So ask and listen.

By trying to be empathetic and stand in others' shoes we can better anticipate the way they'll approach problems and how they'll think about those problems. Best of all it stops you being impatient with them. Sometimes the best technique is to encourage everyone to think out loud as this helps people work together. Blurting out your thoughts in company can get a useful debate going and it's when things are out in the open that it becomes easier to understand them.

Finally business is ultimately pragmatic. It's about getting things done well, done ethically (hopefully always that) and done profitably. To get things done people have to do them. To get them to do them with conviction they need to believe in what they are doing. When Patrick O'Sullivan[6] said this very wise thing he was not saying getting it right didn't matter, he was saying without support and help a decision won't get implemented however right it is:

'It's more important to get buy-in than just make the right decision.'

We all of us spend too much time trying to win little battles of arguments than we spend trying to enrol support for a course everyone can buy into. Only when we actively listen to everyone and try to see it from their point of view do we understand that our own perfect solution, whilst perfect conceptually, may prove, in practice, to be unpopular, cause trouble or be difficult to make happen.

Think about how to build teamwork

In his book *The Five Dysfunctions of the Team* Patrick Lencioni[7] said:

'It is teamwork that remains the ultimate competitive advantage, both because it is so powerful and because it is so rare.'

He praises the humanity of teams:

'...teams succeed because they are exceedingly human.'

Our human imperfections rather than being a source of weakness allow us moments of great creativity and occasionally devastating insights that the smartest algorithm won't begin to comprehend. Dr Bob Rotella, a famous golf coach, wrote a book with a spectacularly wonderful title, *Golf is not a Game of Perfect*.

Nor is life; because life is about conflicting opinions, interests and prejudices. And were empathy a golf club it would be the one we should be using a lot in this game of business life. (Think of empathy as a pitching wedge.)

Teams mystify people. 'The England Team' whether in football, cricket or rugby constantly seem to disappoint their fans and thousands of words are spent lamenting this and wondering why. Watching my grandsons playing football and seeing their reluctance to pass the ball, being intent on scoring themselves, I suspect the 'passing muscle' is one we all need to develop a bit more if teamwork is to improve.

Well run group-thinking meetings, where ideas are passed to and fro, provided these sessions are short, sharp and good humoured, can achieve great things. They can generate ideas, pass on information and bond the team together. But sometimes very clever people in a group can make very stupid decisions. Richard Brown, MD of Cognosis, has created Brown's Law: 'a group's collective intelligence is inversely proportional to the sum of its constituent IQ.'

But, like it or not, we're hard wired to work together and be altruistic. What Haidt, thinking of bees, calls our 'hivish' potential is strong. All we have to ensure is that our team is not just made up of very clever clones. And then we have to play what the Dutch call 'total football'.[8] This idea is very appealing. Imagine a team who work together so well that everyone covers everyone else and the speed of movement is fluidly seamless.

 **tip**

Learn to play the 'total football' version of business – where everyone covers everyone else, playing as a team, passing the ball with seamless understanding.

Notes

1 Marco Iacoboni is Professor of Psychiatry and Biobehavioral Sciences and Director of the Transcranial Magnetic Stimulation Lab at the Ahmanson-Lovelace Brain Mapping Center, Los Angeles.

2 Sam Richards is a sociologist working at the Pennsylvania State University. His work focuses on race and ethnicity. He studied sociology because, he said, it enabled him to learn 'everything about anything'. His TED talk 'A Radical Experiment in Empathy' is the third most watched TED talk ever.

3 Brené Brown is an American scholar, author, and public speaker, who is currently a research professor at the University of Houston Graduate College of Social Work. She is doing ground breaking work into empathy.

4 Deborah Tannen is an American academic and professor of linguistics at Georgetown University in Washington, DC. She has been McGraw Distinguished Lecturer at Princeton University and was a fellow at the Centre for Advanced Study in the Behavioral Sciences following a term in residence at the Institute for Advanced Study in Princeton, NJ. She's a prolific writer of books into empathy and communication.

5 Harold Leavitt (1922–2007) was an American psychologist of management. He dealt with the analysis of patterns of interaction and communication in groups, and also interferences in communication. He examined the personality characteristics of leaders.

6 Patrick O'Sullivan is the Chairman of Old Mutual, Deputy Governor of the Bank of Ireland and Senior Independent Director of Man Group. He is a past Finance Director of Zurich Financial Services Group. He's also a Non-Executive Chairman of the Shareholder Executive – the 'Shareholder Executive's' role is to be the effective shareholder of businesses owned or part-owned by the government and to manage government's interventions in the private sector in order to secure best value for the taxpayer.

7   Patrick Lencioni is an American writer of books on business management, particularly in relation to team management. He previously worked with the consultancy firm Bain. In his various books, which are more like management fables than textbooks, he entertainingly describes modern management challenges.

8   'Total Football' is the label given to an influential tactical theory of football in which any outfield player can take over the role of any other player in a team. It was pioneered by Dutch football club Ajax. In this fluid system, no outfield player is fixed in a nominal role; anyone can successively play as attacker, midfielder and defender. The only player fixed in a nominal position is the goalkeeper. Total Football's tactical success depends largely on the adaptability of each footballer within the team. The theory requires players to be comfortable in multiple positions; hence, it places high technical and physical demands on them.

CHAPTER 14

Ways to connect more effectively

W e all need practical advice on how to create better ways of thinking about other people. Is it a soft skill which in a task-crammed world seems like a nice-to-have or a critical skill that differentiates good companies from bad companies? I think you know what I think.

How to get attention

Getting the attention of others isn't easy because in a world filled with white noise, where there's non-stop advertising and breaking news, attention has become the most precious global commodity. Getting attention matters because you can't interact without it and interacting is the quickest and best way of connecting.

 **tip**

Ask people what they think and the process of empathy is under way.

In one way we are blessed. It's so easy to get information, so easy to find out who did what and when to whom – all this information is just a click away. But there's so much information that it begins to lose its value and it begins to dominate our thinking. John Beedham, a partner at Mercer the consulting firm, says:

'We stop behaving like a human system, spend too much time on data and spend much too little time working with people.'

Getting others to pay attention is really hard so find some key ways to do it.

The more you say something the truer it seems

We advertising people have forever known that 'impacts' matter but even we hadn't realised quite how hardwired the brain is to respond to the fact that people's trust in an assertion grows the more they hear it.

 **tip**

Keep telling the same story. They'll believe it more the more they hear it.

Crisis gets attention

But do be careful of people freezing in the crisis headlights. An old consulting method for activating a supine company used to be to create a fictional crisis on the basis that a crisis gets adrenalin flowing and concentrates the collective corporate mind. In the real world of crises see how well America responded to the floods on the East Coast in 2013 or watch a well-drilled company swing into action on a product recall. But the boy can cry wolf too often and calling 'crisis' just to sharpen up reactions can prove as dangerous as calling 'fire' too often to the fire brigade. Crisis must not become routine.

'Whisper loudly'

Do this in a noisy world because they'll strain to hear what you say. Just matching your noise to the noise of others isn't empathetic, it's crass. In a noisy world putting more value on what you say and how well you say it is the key, not just how much volume you attach to the message. The laconic line attached to the iconic Araldite poster of the 1970s where Araldite glue was used to attach a Ford Cortina to a poster in the Cromwell Road – 'It also sticks handles to teapots' – was a great example of a very loud whisper.

 **tip**

> Speak quietly – it sounds more thoughtful and less threatening. It invites people to listen and reply.

Don't interrupt

To know you'll never be interrupted is a brilliant way of showing a speaker that the listener understands. It places a value on what you have to say. When this is accompanied by a 'keep-talking' voice on the listener's part it can be very productive in getting previously unheard and valuable views to the surface.

How to build self-esteem and self-confidence

I've spoken of the dangers of 'overconfidence' when a group assumes the football hooligan mentality of a chanting, mindless mob – 'here-we-go, here-we-go'. Killer-confident teams usually get an abrupt come-uppance at one time or another and find a reversal of fortunes hard to deal with. Watch the slides in fortune of a BP, Tesco or a Manchester United.

Jack Welch, the one-time boss of General Electric, believed that 'Giving people self-confidence is by far the most important thing that I can do. Because then they will act.'

'I look for speed, simplicity and self-confidence.'

This seems a pretty good statement of cultural need in a modern world. But the distinction is between overconfidence (overbearing, bullying cockiness) and quiet assurance that the available skills are resilient and intelligent enough to cope with anything.

John Scott, who later went on to become HR Director of Lazard's Bank, left his then job to do the journey of a lifetime. To walk the Appalachian Way. This is a story of survival.

The Appalachian way is in the USA. It's over 1200 miles long, it goes through 14 States, in walking it you'll experience over three seasons of the year (pray that you don't over-run and hit winter) and it 'will take' 4–6 months to cover if you can manage to walk 15–20 miles a day… every day. 'Will take' should be re-expressed as 'would take' since few people successfully complete this marathon journey. You are on your own but you are also there to be with, to help and to cajole others whom you meet (and vice versa). They should call this 'The Empathetic Way'. You are on your own but there are fellow travellers out there too. John says you need to help them when required, and sometimes when you are not actually wanted, when you spot something going wrong. You need to be sensitive to the smallest of signals in the body. You need to be caring and ruthless and remember that moving at the speed of the slowest member is not always good enough. You need to understand your own centre of balance and recovery rate and know where your and others' physical and emotional limits lie. To this John rather grimly adds 'even when you or they have actually moved beyond them.'

On this extraordinary trip he learned about himself and others. He learned most of all to observe, not just to see but to observe tell-tale signs. He came to believe in the powerful alliance of self-doubt and self-esteem which beats brains alone in driving yourself and others to a goal. You must remove 'it can't be done because…' from your life but you must also remove 'nothing is impossible…' as a mantra. Because if you don't remove both you'll probably die.

Avoid bad words and phrases and laugh instead

To slightly misquote the 1939 song 'it ain't what you say it's the way that you say it…'. Small nuances and different expressions can transform the way a meeting goes or the sense you communicate to people. Never overestimate your ability to communicate.

Just try any of these phrases to see how they depress people:

> 'But'; 'Mind you'; 'By the way'…; 'Suppose for the sake of argument';
> That's all very well but'; 'So you say'; 'Well anyway'; 'Let's be grown
> up about this'; 'And another thing'; 'Can I get back to you?' or
> the biggest fib of all – another way of saying 'no' – 'Let me think
> about it.'

But there's a positive behaviour that has an enormously positive impact. Humour; humour because it gains attention; people listen to someone who's funny in case they say something that is going to make them laugh; it inspires positive thinking and it acts as an anaesthetic of the mind. You stop thinking about the past when someone's being funny. You live in the present, pleasantly free of extraneous thoughts and stress.

 **tip**

If you want to connect with people avoid negative words like
'but'… . Be positive instead.

Be counsel for the prosecution and defence

We know how hard it is seeing things from different points of view especially understanding what the argument might be against a point of view that you strongly hold. It will help to sharpen your own argument and understand the contrary viewpoint if you try to present two contrary points of view.

 **tip**

Often the best way of understanding an opponent's passionate objections is to build their argument in your own mind and think it through.

Always encourage people to try

We have this dreadful tendency to stick our heads in the sand and hope the presentation or proposal we need to write will go away. We all need people around us who encourage, coach and help us to go for it. The famous Canadian hockey player Wayne Gretzky[1] said: 'You miss 100 per cent of the shots you never make.' Yes, I've used this quote before but the more I read it the truer it seems.

Psychological research suggests that we should coach a race of 'triers' rather than just go talent-spotting for 'high achievers'. People praised for their talent wallow in their superiority until they hit a big problem. People praised for their efforts become hard-wired into believing that the harder they work the better they get. In the 1970s Robin Cousins,[2] in a quest to get even better as an ice skater, went to the USA to be coached. He was dismissively criticised, being told he didn't 'skate to fall'. When he pushed himself beyond the limits he previously settled for he started to win gold.

We need people around us who empathise with our talent and ambition and are smart enough to get inside our heads to release our real innate potential.

Ask the right questions

We are all predisposed to try to get the answers we want to hear. Sometimes (although not often) this is justified. When the ground-breaking advertising for VW, originally created by Doyle Dane Bernbach, was researched in the USA it did badly. When asked what he thought about this Bill Bernbach said: 'Get me some more research.' Generally we are reticent in soliciting people's opinions. And it's less important to know whether they think 'yes' or 'no' than in more general terms what's on their minds. They seldom know exactly what they want, they usually misread the new brand (recall those cavemen when asked what they thought of the fire and the wheel) but their mood matters. So ask their opinions. Do surveys.

 **tip**

People seldom know what they want. They have vague feelings. If we understand these, we'll give them what they need but can't articulate.

In business, politics resides not in trying to manoeuvre and twist and turn and play the 'game', but in understanding what the general swing of thinking about any number of issues is. So e-mail senior people and beg a favour of them – find out what they really think. People are wonderfully candid. Don't double guess when you don't need to. Finally stop worrying about what other people think about you and instead focus on working pragmatically with what a one-time, well-known politician called R.A. Butler described as the 'art of the possible'.[3] Do not invest too much time in projects that will be very difficult to get through. These projects may be right or even brilliant but their time may not be right.

How to create the right environment

In researching this book I've been surprised by the hostility that HR provokes even, this most strangely, amongst HR people. I was told that 'empathetic HR' is oxymoronic, that HR people are not good at nor especially concerned about what people think. Some went further in their candour saying HR is 'crap' because they set out to do what managers should do.

My own take on the best HR people I know is rather different. Jack Welch thought HR and finance – getting the people right and the money right – was the groundwork on which vision and strategy could flourish. My own favourite definition is the HR Director from Canada who said her role was as 'casting director'.

Some HR practices seem pretty counterproductive. I do not much like categorising people in the Myers Briggs way. Anne Gillies who earned her reputation at the 'people friendly' W.L. Gore and Associates said: 'If you trust people they'll do a good job.' And it's especially so in a business which focuses on creating small, independent, operational cells rather than in building a matricised, structural edifice. It's in those that dissatisfaction is rife.

Towers Watson, who do major job satisfaction surveys, did one globally in 2007–08 (not the best years to choose perhaps) among 90,000 respondents worldwide. Some 38 per cent of workers claimed they were completely disengaged. This would tend to suggest either terrible management or a world where trying to engage workers was not treated seriously.

Someone has to champion the stuff that makes a difference – better spaces that are quiet, light, comfortable, have good locations and views, are friendly to the idea of providing abundant stimuli and with good access to practical stuff, because if our teams can't concentrate they can't reflect deeply or, probably, reflect at all. If this isn't a primary focus of HR – our people engineers – then I agree with the HR naysayers.

 tip

In our quest to understand people so we can empathise with them it's essential to see them as relaxed people, off duty and at home.

I've already referred to a comparative test – HR experts versus psychological researchers – the latter outscored the former who studied CVs in their assessment and understanding of potential candidates as opposed to the researchers who went to candidates' flats to snoop around. Real experience always beats theory.

Why are we so bad at internal communications?

We spend large sums communicating with our consumers and our trade customers but very little with our workforce, and what we do spent is usually badly thought out. How is it that our style of talking to them most resembles the sort of propaganda seen in the First World War – remember that Kitchener recruitment poster 'Your country needs you'? It may have been OK then, now it just looks old-fashioned, patronising and ill thought through.

If we want to be the sort of company that gets the best out of our people by listening to them we would address communications urgently.

 tip

When teams think their opinion is respected they just tend to try a little harder.

Brilliant ways of reaching people include:

- **Mentoring**. Coaching people to do their jobs better, addressing their weaknesses so they become more self-aware works and improves thinking skills.

- **Eyeball contact.** Technology makes life easier. Teleconferencing and videoconferencing are very useful aids but when people tell me they've cut their event and travel bill so this is the only way of meeting their peers around the country and the world nowadays, I wince. Face-to-face time is essential to a thinking company.

- **Magic tools**. Space, simple English, and style. Every office needs a 'space' for people to be together... a coffee bar or sitting room. Executives need to talk in English rather than jargon. And people need to demonstrate they 'care' by demonstrating a little style. Companies like Shine, Google or Abbott Mead Vickers are good at this. How they create internal events is part of their branding strategy.

- **Coffee.** 'Science may never come up with a better method of communication than the coffee break.' This appeared as a message on the wall in the Royal Institute. It's true.

- **Social media**. It has a big role to play. It's never been easier to share news, thoughts and reminders than on social media. This is the generation of sharing. Use the technology that makes this not only easy but also free.

Sense the difference

In being empathetic we are not being calculating. We are relying on our ability to put ourselves in another's position so as to feel (or sense) how they feel as well as how they think. It's not a feeling that we can feel all the time. It calls, instead, for a certain effort of will.

 **tip**

We need to feel how others feel not just to think how others think. Empathy requires imagination.

Importantly we need to realise that whilst we have five obvious senses there are a lot more. It's this vein of thinking that leads us to conclude that the human brain is not just hard to get our minds round. It's distinctly extraordinary. Because not only do we have other senses we also have satellites of our brains in our stomach, heart and other parts of the anatomy. In our stomach, for instance, complex work is under the control of what's sometimes called 'the little brain', a network of neurons that line your stomach and your gut. Surprisingly, there are over 100 million of these cells in your gut, as many as there are in the head of a cat. The little brain does not do a lot of complex thinking but it does get on with the daily grind involved in digesting food. This involves lots of mixing, contracting and absorbing, to help break down our food and begin extracting the nutrients and vitamins that we need.

There are various different kinds of being smart which when you think about it raises questions about an educational system that focuses on just the three 'R's. There's the smartness attached to logic; words; pictures; music; to your body and to people. Few are good at all of them. But for sure your ability to think empathetically will be impaired if you don't have 'people-smarts'.

We also have more than five senses. Technically some of these are rather loosely conceived but indulge me because the point is this – the senses are what our system 1 does. They are our intuition. And I love the idea of common sense, a sense of fun, a sense of love or sense of premonition:

- common sense – the instinct to do the right and sensible thing;

- 'gut feeling' (which includes the sense of premonition) – the sense of something being right or not right (this is the intuition that Malcolm Gladwell writes about in *Blink*);
- sense of balance;
- sense of love or 'caritas' which carries the sense of altruism with it. (Altruism of course is the most empathetic of all the human characteristics, when putting others above self is the key.)
- sense of temperature;
- kinaesthetics or the sense of direction – what allegedly men have and women lack;
- a sense of body space – close your eyes and touch the end of your nose, yes, that sense.

brilliant tip

In a piece of machinery as complicated as a human, not trying to understand the feelings of others isn't just remiss – it's very unwise.

Notes

1   Wayne Gretzky is a Canadian former professional ice hockey player. He played 20 seasons in the National Hockey League (NHL) for four teams from 1979 to 1999. Nicknamed 'The Great One', he has been called 'the greatest hockey player ever' by many sportswriters, players, and the NHL itself. He is the leading point-scorer in NHL history.

2   Robin Cousins is a British former competitive figure skater. He was the 1980 Olympic champion, the 1980 European champion, a three-time World medallist and four-time British national champion. He later starred in ice shows and also produced his own.

3   R. A. Butler, 1902–82, familiarly known as 'Rab', was a British Conservative politician. Butler was one of only two British

politicians to have served in three of the four Great Offices of State (Chancellor of the Exchequer, Home Secretary and Foreign Secretary) but never to have been Prime Minister, for which he was twice passed over.

CHAPTER 15

Understanding changing minds and changing times

The world is changing. The way people behave is changing too, as is their attitudes to a variety of issues, especially how we treat each other. The sort of people who run companies is changing. More women, more people from different cultures, more young people and cleverer people carrying less baggage than those from 'old Britain'. It's time to understand this new world.

Understand these life-critical stereotypes: men and women

I was thinking how strange it seems to even raise the subject of men and women, to say they're different and how important it is to treat the contribution that women make more seriously. I mean, seriously, this is the 21st century. Isn't it obvious? Apparently not as books like the *Confidence Code*,[1] a handbook to enhance female self-confidence in the workplace, continue to be so popular. And what worries me about such books is rather than celebrating the fact that women have different strengths they tend to aim at making women more masculine to compete in a man's world.

It isn't a man's world any more is it?

It was October 2010 and I'd been invited by someone I was coaching to Mercers in the Marsh McLellan building over-looking the Tower of London for an evening conference called the 'Power of Women'. I was one of seven men in an audience of a hundred. The other men seemed to not want to be there and appeared to be misogynists. I behaved rather badly, calling one of them a dinosaur. We nearly came to blows I recall; very playground stuff. The key speaker was Margaret Heffernan who'd written the unfortunately titled *Women on Top*.[2] She and a panel of women including Kirstin Furber, HR Head of BBC Worldwide, explained some of the differences between women and men. They helped explain why in the USA women had a much better track record at starting businesses than men (and why women of colour were even more likely to succeed). The list of attributes described was impressively long:

- Women are more motivated – they take a long time deciding to do it and when they do wholeheartedly go for it.
- They want to build a sustainable business not just get rich.
- Their sense of the zeitgeist is profound – men go from A to Z in a purposeful straight line. Women tend to wander and pick up useful information as they do so, informing their sense of what's on other people's minds.
- They recognise patterns better than men.
- They are team players and builders and embrace diversity.
- They aren't so target obsessed – men always seem to want business plans, failing to recognise that creating a spreadsheet doesn't make it true.
- They use their instincts more comfortably – men like to think they are logical, analytical and emotion-free decision machines.
- They tell the truth more readily because they realise saying 'I'm sorry it was my fault' is more convincing than 'the dog ate my homework'.

Alan and Barbara Pease wrote *Why Men Don't Listen and Women Can't Read Maps*, which is on the same theme. Psychological research shows men and women who score pretty much the same in an IQ test, score very differently when a monetary incentive is applied to the result with men surging ahead. Evidence shows men tend to hire in their own image and believe in transactions and 'leadership'. Women tend to believe in relationships and teamwork.

Christine Lagarde[3] – together with Angela Merkel, the German Chancellor, the most impressive role models for women today – said in the 2014 Richard Dimbleby lecture, 'A New Multilateralism for the 21st Century':

> 'Women talk emotively. Men are literal. Boys like things. Girls like people. Girls co-operate. Men hate to be wrong.'

Maybe we all need to pay attention a bit more carefully to these strengths and differences.

A generation apart or an opportunity?

When I look at generations Y and Z I think how lucky we are. The brighter of the new generations are nicer, smarter and more adaptable than those who went before. They are global citizens and the rites of passage their parents went through like planning a career, passing the driving test and getting on the property ladder seem to many a bit outdated. In focusing on the under 30 year olds I run into the danger of wild stereotyping yet we should think about these characteristics and trends. They are encouraging and liberating.

This is the 'keep your possessions to a very high quality minimum generation'; the first genuinely paper-free generation, the mortgage free, virtual office generation; and the get on a plane to go where it takes you at a moment's notice generation. They look at quality and quantity together. How many shoes do you have? How many do you really need? OK a pair of great trainers, a pair of great loafers. Two pairs of great jeans. Two wonderful shirts, two great T-shirts. iPad, iPod. And so on and so on or rather – not so on and so on.

Choose your best brands, the ones that market to your true sense of yourself – Boss, Armani, Gucci, whoever – and have what you need for the only reality there is: the reality of now. Don't store up mediocrity of product for a rainy day. Wear only the best now. And throw or give it away when you need to replace it.

Welcome to generation Y and Z.

If a brand is not cool, crafted and quality it's in trouble. Marketing is a start but not enough. This generation demands fashion but also fashion that doesn't fall apart. It knows not only how to complain but how to get reparation. If you don't supply them with great customer service they'll lash you on the web.

 **tip**

For generation Y and Z what really matters now is what their peers think and say not what marketers tell them.

The only 'proper job' will be one you enjoy and learn from. Most likely you will work for yourself or be freelance. You will be a talent not an employee. You will hone your skills so they are world class. They won't just be transferable – they'll be transferable across continents. And you'll only do what you want to do and what makes you better. Money will be secondary.

They drink little alcohol, less than any preceding generations, drugs have stopped being cool and teenage and early twenties unexpected pregnancy is a thing of the distant past. They are quite serious and much better behaved than young people used to be. Responsible is their middle name.

Their minds have been changed by years of computer games so they think they can multitask and have low boredom thresholds. They aren't being intentionally rude when they switch off but if it's a dull presentation, it's dull and the presenter should get over it. They are great communicators at a low level of observation, saying 'hey did you know/have you seen/have you heard?' They are electronic gossips. They absorb and discard very quickly. They have masses of friends and acquaintances. This is the network generation.

This generation will demand from its employers, stakeholders, partners and suppliers:

- transparency,
- innovation,
- care for the environment,
- care for the community,
- diversity,
- relationships not just transactions.

The workforce of the future won't go on strike if dissatisfied – they'll just walk out – forever. The old-fashioned command/control model has already died; the new 'Z-model' is about teams and talent with a premium on task-delivery; on creating a great film/programme or a great new fashion line or a great event. Generation Z won't be adversarial they'll simply be impervious to that employer ordering do it my way nonsense.

brilliant tip

Generation Y and Z are the 'thinking generations'. They are high achievers and use their brains to succeed.

It's this last observation that is of course the most thrilling. They are collectively going to be the most frightening electorate for any politician. They will think about what they're hearing and if they don't like it they'll not vote at all or vote en masse to make a point. Expect more shocks.

People are changing: expectations are changing

Back to the altrocentric leader, back to thinking about others and not just ourselves. We can expect all sorts of changes driven by cultural integration and by an across the board rise in global service standards. Amazon raises the bar, restaurants raise the bar and employees are forcing employers to raise the bar. As Nancy Kline says:

 'In changing times everyone has to be on their thinking mettle.'

If you can really get into other people's minds and think about them you'll be successful at marketing to them and great at managing them. Understanding and working with people is the biggest skill there is. It's the thinking skill that will increasingly be regarded as the greatest business asset there is. Bullies of the future quake because it's game over for you.

Notes

1   *The Confidence Code*, by journalists Katty Kay and Claire Shipman, looks at the neuroscience of female confidence and seeks the confidence gene. They talk to leading psychologists who explain how women can choose to become more confident simply by taking action and courting risk, and how those actions change the brain's wiring.

2   Margaret Heffernan is an entrepreneur, author and CEO. After working for the BBC as a producer, she started and ran five media and high-tech businesses in the USA. She discovered that women are more values-oriented, more flexible, and less ego-driven than

their male counterparts; as a result they're creating, she believes, company cultures that are better able to meet the demands of the new economy.

3   Christine Lagarde is a French lawyer and politician who has been the Managing Director of the International Monetary Fund since 2011. Previously, she held various ministerial posts in the French government. She was the first woman to become finance minister of a G8 economy and is the first woman to head the IMF.

PART 7

Final thoughts

CHAPTER 16

Using our minds to their full potential

'Stop and think.' By now you've got a lot of material to think about but what follows are the don't leave home without them tips and parting thoughts. The human brain is in the news almost every day. Neuroscientists are learning more, new treatments for dementia are being discovered, we are thinking about 'thinking' much more and much harder than we have since the Greek philosophers were puzzling away.

Beware!

Sometimes we think that we think better than we do.

In business there are top teams who think they have a strategy but don't. We all of us think we think, but we are in Action Man mode most of the time, doing deals, clinching sales, producing reports. Thinking is the last thing on our mind.

 **tip**

Keep asking yourself 'What do I think?' and 'What do I really think?' And then ask other people 'What do *you* think?'

Why (hopefully) this book matters is that it's trying to help people think more carefully, more thoroughly, more creatively and more constructively.

Understand our thinking limitations

We all understand about systems 1 and 2 – the intuitive mind and the rational mind. We also understand that the intuitive mind is the powerhouse, that this drives all our thinking. System 2, the rational brain, is weaker and lazier.

 **tip**

What we have to do is to achieve a better balance when we think. Prod the rational brain the whole time to keep up.

Think about it as having two counsellors in your head… a funny, impulsive, opinionated one and a clever, calculating, cautious one. Get both of them working, not just the charismatic counsellor. Jonathan Haidt in *The Righteous Mind* put it like this. There's a man sitting on an elephant. The man is system 2. He's smart and astute, being carried along by the mighty elephant – that's system 1 – who'll pay attention to him but sometimes just has his own way.

Whichever metaphor you prefer, use it. To think properly we need to know there's a conversation going on in our heads and work out how to get the best out of our thinking counsellors. Keep on testing the thoughts you have… do they add up and do they make sense? Quite simply train your brain to think harder.

Beware of these thinking traps

There are a series of thinking traps which can prevent us thinking straight. All we have to do is constantly question if we are slipping into a trap:

- **Prejudgement** – have we made up our mind before listening to the evidence?

- **Force fitting** – are we trying to force fit this problem so it resembles something similar that we think we know how to solve?

- **Rewriting the brief** – beware, because we don't even notice ourselves doing this, changing the brief to one we'd prefer to answer.

- **Seduced by appearances** – we can be highly influenced by appearances and prefer what good-looking people tell us in nice places.

- **Beguiled by success** – 'I've done something similar before and won'… now how did it go?

- **Having a pet interest** – also called 'emotional tagging' – irrational resistance to changing something or a belief that what you like is right.

- **Being ego-defensive** – 'this is my territory and (however irrational) I'm going to defend it'.

- **Being entitlement focused** – 'I'm owed or I deserve or it isn't fair I haven't got …'.

- **Being inflexible** – 'because we've already decided we can't change' – this is common in big corporations where often a board decision can't be changed even when wrong.

- **Being fossilised and bureaucratic** – 'we always do it this way'.

- **Being lazy** – 'whatever…' – that's the retort of the inert brain. It's when you don't have the energy to think it through or simply that you've lost interest.

The laws of business that always apply however hard we think

In a way it's comforting to know that history always repeats itself and that humans are always going to behave in inconsistent, mercurial and irrational ways. Here are the big ones:

- Alchemy doesn't work – but we keep on hoping it will.
- Nothing survives forever – things have to change.
- Every reward has an opposing risk – but you seldom hear the downside.
- Stupid behaviour is catching.

 **tip**

> Be phlegmatic. Life's unfair. They keep moving the goalposts. You can only try your best.

The four thinking systems

Problem-solving

This is where you've got to get your system 2 to work. Well Mr/Mrs Rational 'what do you think?' Brief? Evidence? Research? Opinions of those close to the problem? Personal observation? More research? What are the options? Problem-solving needs a fully functioning brain, a solid process and an appetite to find good solutions – that's all.

Decision-making

All decisions are to some extent gambles. We'll never have all the evidence. We need to make as well informed a guess as we can. The best we can do is to be thoroughly briefed, listen carefully to all the arguments, maintain an above the battle view and delay making a decision prematurely. A fast decision is seldom a good one unless your intuition is shrieking 'watch out' because if it is, pay heed to that voice. Finally having made the decision make sure it's followed through and executed. Bad execution is the cause of most business problems.

Creative thinking

'The game-changer' – this the way in which you can truly out-flank your competitors. Get in the right mood and embrace that blank sheet of paper like new clothes. Remove those 'I can't' blocks. Always think customer first. Always look for little ways to improve everything. Be a bit of a rebel. Use creative exercises to stretch your creative mind. Create workshops that everyone wants to come to. This is where system 1 comes into its own. Go on, surprise yourself.

Thinking how others think

This is the key to great management and getting things done. Thinking and feeling how others think and feel will mean your communications will reach them. We don't listen enough. We interrupt. We underestimate how well-meaning most people actually want to be. Understanding people is the key to the 21st century. So start listening very carefully.

 'All business decisions are marketing decisions, all marketing decisions are about people.'

Martin Sorrell

Magic questions

Why, what, how, when, where, how much?

Using these questions will unearth the key ingredients for a robust, thoughtful and creative solution. Becoming a gentle but persistent questioner and an attentive listener will take you a long way as a thinker.

 tip

Finding out what you need to know will happen if you learn how to ask the right questions. And keep asking until you find out what you want.

Your memory is a very powerful tool

Pushing yourself to use Sherlock Holmes' energy, focus and interrogative attitude to solve problems can transform the power and depth of your thinking. The fact is that we all know more than we think we know. The only problem with Sherlock was his complete absence of emotional intelligence. But that mind-palace memory is something to envy. Mind-mapping is a powerful way of stretching our minds and the greater our sense of curiosity the better our memories will be. That's why stories are so popular; they're easy to remember.

Reach: how far can we go as thinkers?

I'd guess most of us are operating at less than 50 per cent of our thinking capacity. If this was your body we were considering as opposed to your mind we'd be tut-tutting and putting you on a strict diet and a series of punishing work-out exercises.

Examining the level of change we can achieve and how to bench-mark our thinking skills can only be achieved by asking three questions:

● Are we rigorously practising ways of thinking better?

● Do we recognise that hard thinking is demanding, calorie-devouring work?

● Do we understand how wonderfully versatile, clever and imaginative our brains are?

The answer to all these should, by now, be categorically 'yes'. We can deal with the problem of tweets, data-overload and bullet points which can make life seem a bit simplistic and trivial. Let's set ourselves higher standards of rigour. There's nothing wrong with occasional junk food or Twitter or Mars Bars. But you can't live only on those. In a complex world we need to train our brains to think more cleverly. It's the only way to stay ahead and move things forward.

Just when you think you've cracked it someone moves one of the pieces and you're back to square one. But we can, if we work at it, outwit competitors and think of new ways to win.

All you need is a clean sheet of paper, a sharp pencil and the right attitude. Try this from Steve Jobs, to conclude, for advice:

 'My mantras are focus and simplicity. Simple can be harder than complex: You have to work hard to get your thinking clean to make it simple.'

But it's what he says next that I like most:

 'It's worth it in the end because once you get there, you can move mountains.'

Go now and move some mountains. Good luck.

A reading list

These are just a few of the books I've read and more specifically picked up and read again while writing this book. What's daunting is how many good minds there are out there. Thank you ladies and gentlemen for making my research so much fun. Don't stop thinking good thoughts.

Allan, Dave, Kingdon, Matt, Murrin, Kris and Rudkin, Daz
?WhatIf! How to Start a Creative Revolution at Work Capstone (19 April 2002)
More of a sales brochure for their business than anything else but, nonetheless, some interesting and stimulating ideas.

Bourdain, Anthony
Les Halles Cookbook: Classic Bistro Cooking Bloomsbury Publishing PLC (4 September 2006)
I thought I'd bought a cookbook and found I was getting a brilliant education in how to run a creative business and one that's under constant pressure. Pure genius.

Brafman, Ori and Beckstrom, Rod
The Starfish and the Spider: The Unstoppable Power of Leaderless Organizations Portfolio (5 October 2006)
Bill Clinton said this was one of his most thought provoking books. It puts the skids under the concept of the CEO – 'who's CEO of the internet then… go on tell me who, there must be one – surely?' It's a great read.

Broughton, Philip Delves

What They Teach You at Harvard Business School: My Two Years Inside the Cauldron of Capitalism Penguin (7 May 2009)

He's a nice guy in a really horrible, left-brained place that I hated the more I read about it. Yet his adventure is a splendidly told story. He was the only one not offered a job after graduating from HBS that year. I was so pleased that he was spared to write this educational and funny epic.

Catmull, Ed

Creativity, Inc.: Overcoming the Unseen Forces That Stand in the Way of True Inspiration Bantam Press (8 April 2014)

There are bits here that are great. About believing you should make a film that *you* want to watch as other people might then want to watch it too, about art classes being to do with learning to see not learning to draw, about the randomness of business life and about the need to try new things constantly.

Chouinard, Yvon

Let My People Go Surfing: The Education of a Reluctant Businessman Penguin Press (6 October 2005)

A fascinating story about a successful company called Patagonia, the focus of which was very narrow in terms of sector and fixed like a laser on great product quality. The conviction about working with people you like and trust and staying true to your values resonated.

Collins, Jim

Good to Great Random House Business (4 October 2001)

When I first read this book with its carefully worked out score-cards-for-success I was impressed. I found the concept of the self-effacing team-building leader seductive. As time has passed and chaos has increasingly reigned nothing seems that simple any more.

Davis, Stan and Mayer, Christopher

Blur: The Speed of Change in Connected Economy Capstone (1 September 1999)

Yes I know... a bit old by now as an insight into technology but this was the first book I came across that put its finger on the increasing speed of the pulse of today's world.

De Bono, Edward

Serious Creativity: Using the Power of Lateral Thinking to Create New Ideas HarperCollins (10 April 1995)

Six Thinking Hats Penguin (5 November 2009)

De Bono is the Daddy of writing on creativity. I'm not sure I go along with his attitude to creativity or his regimented approach but it would be remiss not to consult his fine mind.

Dennett, Daniel C.

Intuition Pumps and other Tools for Thinking Penguin (6 May 2013)

Until he got on to the maths in this book, which lost me a bit, I thought it was amazing. He sits next to the late Christopher Hitchens and Richard Dawkins as a formidable contrarian. If you want OPINION look no further.

Finkelstein, Sydney, Whitehead, Jo and Campbell, Andrew

Think Again: Why Good Leaders Make Bad Decisions and How to Keep it From Happening to You Harvard Business Review Press (3 February 2009)

Marcus Alexander recommended this as he knows Whitehead and Campbell. It's fascinating as an exercise in hindsight and closely examining the way the business mind – forensic as we hope it is – drifts hopelessly into bias and subjectivity given the slightest chance.

Friedman, Thomas

The World is Flat: The Globalized World in the Twenty-first Century Penguin (5 July 2007)

Friedman is a brilliant observer of human nature and above all keeps his finger on the pulse of the global-socio-economic body. It's above the battle and with his sleeves rolled up both at the same time. Stirring stuff.

Gladwell, Malcolm

Blink: The Power of Thinking Without Thinking Penguin (23 February 2006)

David and Goliath: Underdogs, Misfits and the Art of Battling Giants Penguin (8 May 2014)

What the Dog Saw: and Other Adventures Penguin (20 October 2009)

Outliers: The Story of Success Penguin (18 November 2008)

The Tipping Point: How Little Things Can Make a Big Difference Abacus (14 February 2002)

If you are in business and don't read every bit of Gladwell you can lay your hands on then you're missing out. He's a master storyteller and he opens minds. *Blink* and the art of training your gut was a revelatory big thought when it came out and has influenced my book. Gladwell makes you think. We're waiting for the next one.

Haidt, Jonathan

The Righteous Mind: Why Good People are Divided by Politics and Religion Allen Lane (2010)

Not an easy book but it informed much of my thinking especially when he tells us he didn't have the self-confidence to trust his intuition when he was at university. Read it and you get to understand why it is that people don't get on and why this is normal and usually triggered by small things.

Hall, Doug

Jump Start Your Business Brain: Scientific Ideas and Advice That Will Immediately Double Your Business Success Rate Clerisy Press (11 February 2010)

No relation to me, Doug is a product inventor who now runs the 'Eureka Ranch'. I didn't like the book. I found the section on left and right brains simplistic and irritating: 'logical left brains are easier to work with than radical right brains'. Hmmm. But it's sold loads of copies and he's fêted in the States. So pay no attention to me.

Hamel, Gary

What Matters Now: How to Win in a World of Relentless Change, Ferocious Competition, and Unstoppable Innovation Jossey-Bass (4 January 2012)

This book is an impassioned plea to change the way we think about and manage business. He berates the ignorance, indifference and impotence which so many of us accept as OK. He carries on where Tom Peters left off. He ends his book by saying 'we have the chance to make a new beginning'. Halleluya.

Hartigan, Elkington

The Power of Unreasonable People: How Social Entrepreneurs Create Markets That Change the World (Leadership for the Common Good) Harvard Business School Press (1 February 2008)

Much is about how to be a small, social entrepreneur. We see that the power of driving change is thriving in the rural third world. If they can do it there, first world organisations should be ashamed to find it hard to transform themselves. An anthem to passion, change and improvement.

Hoeckin, Lisa

Managing Cultural Differences: Strategies for Competitive Advantage FT PrenticeHall (17 November 1995)

I suspect in 20 years the barriers to cultural integration have somewhat broken down. But this book is a healthy prompt to thinking about global businesses and how different national cultures feel, think and behave.

Isaacson, Walter

Steve Jobs Little, Brown (24 October 2011)

This is the best biography I've read for ages and one the most insightful business books. Warts and all we begin to understand what drove Jobs and how he drove Apple. Warts and all it's a compelling book.

Kahneman, Daniel

Thinking, Fast and Slow Penguin (10 May 2012)

This book defines and shapes a lot of current thinking about thinking. Hard to write anything about the subject without asking what Daniel – Nobel Prize Winner – thinks about it. It's a difficult, dense book that's nonetheless sold millions and has been widely acclaimed as a masterpiece. System 1 and system 2 shapes all we think now. And if I ever meet a woman called Linda I'm walking away from her (read the book and see why).

Kahney, Leander

Inside Steve's Brain: Business Lessons from Steve Jobs, the Man Who Saved Apple Atlantic Books (1 May 2010)

Kahney was an Apple fan and follower for years and whilst this is a eulogy of how Steve 'put a ding in the universe' he also tells how he lent his eye to every detail. What the book lacks in perspective it makes up for in drenching us in the passion everyone at Apple had in trying to do something extraordinary.

Kline, Nancy

Time to Think: Listening to Ignite the Human Mind Cassell Illustrated (1 January 1999)

Nancy has that kind of calm, kind and reasonable voice that drives some people mad. Yet in this book she writes most winningly about empathy and getting people to reveal how they really feel. Whilst reading it I decided to stop interrupting and to listen more attentively. My wife looked at me suspiciously and asked if I was feeling all right.

Konnikova, Maria

Mastermind: How to Think Like Sherlock Holmes Canongate Books (17 January 2013)

Maria is Russian and when small her father read Sherlock Holmes stories to her. Mostly, though, she was brought up in America. She writes with a breathless and fluent energy. Her work is entertaining and whilst covering the more conventional thinking on thinking is especially good on memory – 'the dynamic attic'. A great read.

Kreitzman, Leon

The 24 Hour Society Profile Books (14 October 1999)

The Rhythms of Life: The Biological Clocks That Control the Daily Lives of Every Living Thing (written with Professor Russell Foster) Profile Books (30 September 2011)

Leon, who used to be at the Henley Centre, has an inquisitive and thoughtful mind and whether writing on time or deeply programmed instincts is always a compelling read. After Kreitzman's been telling you engagingly about bees your respect for the brilliance of that species soars.

Lencioni, Patrick

The Five Dysfunctions of a Team: A Leadership Fable Jossey-Bass (17 November 2011)

Lencioni has now written 12 highly readable 'fables'. They're short, punchy and fun. This one examines the make-up of a diverse team, the conflicts and hidden issues. If you don't feel impelled to bone up on your empathetic skills after reading it I'd be surprised.

Levine, Rick *et al.*

The Cluetrain Manifesto Basic Books (2 July 2009)

Four angry guys who just aren't 'going to take it anymore'. It's a brilliant put-down of corporate blah-blah and an impassioned plea for conversations. The consumer after all is not stupid.

Levitt, Steve and Dubner, Stephen

Freakonomics: A Rogue Economist Explores the Hidden Side of Everything Penguin (5 October 2006)

Superfreakonomics: Global Cooling, Patriotic Prostitutes and Why Suicide Bombers Should Buy Life Insurance Penguin (24 June 2010)

Think Like a Freak: How to Think Smarter about Almost Everything Penguin (13 May 2014)

Levitt and Dubner are like two highly intellectual stand-up comedians. Economics and sociology becomes fun in their writing. They think in an optimistically offbeat and contrarian way and provoke us all to look at life sideways because it's never quite what it seems.

Lewis, Dr David

Impulse: Why We Do What We Do Without Knowing Why We Do It Cornerstone Digital (16 May 2013)

All about that 'zombie brain' which unconsciously processes all we do. From adolescence to sex to diet to shopping Lewis shows that we don't make up our minds, our zombie brain does. Interesting stuff.

Lindstrom, Martin

Brandwashed: Tricks Companies Use to Manipulate Our Minds and Persuade Us to Buy Kogan Page (3 January 2012)

Buyology: Truth and Lies about Why We Buy Broadway Business (2 Febrary 2010)

My problem is I just don't accept that marketing is not nowadays a game which consenting human beings play together. Described by some as a marketing visionary, Martin Lindstrom takes us through the research processes of say Lynx – a male fantasy is apparently to be adored by four beautiful naked women – *quelle surprise* that! It's fun and it's thought-provoking but, as he concludes, he (and I) still love brands however salacious his findings.

Martinez-Conde, Susana and Macknik, Stephen

Sleights of Mind: What the neuroscience of magic reveals about our brains Profile Books Ltd. (2 February 2011)

Two married psychologists who go to Las Vegas to try and learn the arts of magic and understand how the human mind welcomes being deceived by magical tricks. It's a wonderful story behind the scenes and an instructive read. I'll never trust a magician again.

Mayer-Schönberger, Viktor and Cukier, Kenneth

Big Data: A Revolution That Will Transform How We Live, Work and Think John Murray (14 March 2013)

I thought I was going to hate this. I was wrong. Read it. From a new view on sampling (where n = everyone) to a sophisticated take on accuracy (where 2 + 2 = 3.9 is good enough) to the story of how the World Health Organisation cracked Avian Flu thanks to Google, I was riveted. This book is very good news to those who want quantification and not just anecdote.

McInnes, Tom

Culture Shock: A Handbook For 21st Century Business Capstone (26 July 2012)

If you like 'angry' you'll love this. Tom passionately believes organisations today desperately need a higher purpose than just gaining market share and profits. He is a king of CSR. Watch the sparks fly.

Morgan, Adam

Eating the Big Fish: How Challenger Brands Can Compete Against Brand Leaders Wiley (3 March 2009)

Impressively assured insights into the beginnings of new marketing where ideas rather than communications are the new currency of growth. I love the idea that staying number one means needing to think like number two.

O'Rourke, P.J.

The CEO of the Sofa Picador (20 September 2002)

The Baby Boom: How It Got That Way… And It Wasn't My Fault And I'll Never Do It Again Grove Press/Atlantic Monthly Press (6 March 2013)

He's funny and outrageous and keeps on hitting the bull's eye. From seeing the resemblance between CEOs and two-year-olds (attention seeking, focused on food and drink, prone to tantrums) to describing how the most liberal generation ever have now become the most anally retentive. Thoughtful, amusing and important stuff.

Peters, Dr Steve

The Chimp Paradox: The Mind Management Programme for Confidence, Success and Happiness Vermillion (5 January 2012)

Dave Brailsford, who's Performance Director of British Cycling, says Peters, who's a sports psychologist, is a 'genius'. This book describes graphically how the mind works with the 'Chimp' a fictional player in System One who's a paranoid, destructive adolescent force imagining what's worst and most unfair. Peters shows us how to control him.

Peters, Tom

Re-Imagine Dorling Kindersley (1 July 2009)

The Circle of Innovation: You Can't Shrink Your Way to Greatness Hodder Headline Australia (11 November 1997)

The passionate Mr Peters bestrode the presentation stage for decades. He's another very angry man who wanted to change everything. A believer in creative destruction. Particularly acute on creative thinking. Wearing a little thin now perhaps.

Ridley, Matt

The Rational Optimist: How Prosperity Evolves Fourth Estate (27 May 2010)

Lord Ridley – scientist and one time banker – is a glass half full person who believes we are going through the best phase of civilisation ever. It's interesting to read a passionate system 2, right brain thinker for a change. Lots of good material here.

Robinson, Sir Kenneth

The Element: How Finding Your Passion Changes Everything Penguin (5 February 2009)

In his TED talk 'Do schools kill creativity' which has so far had over 27 million hits, Ken inspired and entertained us. This book proclaims the power of positivity and focusing on spending your life doing what you love. It's a compelling challenge to corporate business and convention.

Sinclair, Michael and Seydel, Josie

Mindfulness for Busy People: Turning from Frantic and Frazzled into Calm and Composed Pearson Business (26 September 2013)

Mindfulness has been widely espoused, even at Davos. It is, we hear, the 'new black'. This book is full of good advice but managed to irritate me. If only life were this simple. If only they didn't sound so smug.

Surowtecki, James

The Wisdom of Crowds: Why the Many Are Smarter Than the Few Abacus (3 March 2005)

A fascinating story about why the collective views about almost anything when averaged tend to be about right. These include guessing the weight of an ox and the whereabouts of a lost submarine. A tribute to diversity and teamwork.

Syed, Matthew

Bounce: The Myth of Talent and the Power of Practice Harper (20 April 2010)

Matthew was England's number one table tennis player for many years. Like Gladwell's *Outliers* he writes in praise of practice. He tells the story of three sisters who were all coached to be world class chess players and of Desmond Douglas the table tennis player whose earliest practice in a very small space put all the premium on his ability to anticipate. A great read.

Taleb, Nassim Nicholas

Antifragile: Things that Gain from Disorder Allen Lane (27 November 2012)

I loved this book. Taleb is a very cross contrarian who regards economists, bankers, doctors and marketing people as virtually criminal. His thesis is there are things that thrive in disorder, that nature can do well in the face of destruction. Most of all he sends an Exocet missile through the concept of predictions and patterns. More than we imagine is random. Less is predictable. Brilliant.

Thaler, Richard and Sunstein, Cass

Nudge: Improving Decisions About Health, Wealth, and Happiness Yale University Press (13 May 2008)

The idea that we can design a world in which people make better informed and smarter decisions is interesting and it has certainly interested governments. Nudging behavioural change rather than seeking wholesale change of attitude could be a big money-saver.

Thomas, Martin

Loose: The Future of Business is Letting Go Business Plus (3 March 2011)

Like the *Starfish and the Spider* this proclaims the weakness in command control models. Thomas looks at the weakening of political structures, of trust in institutions and of rules – like over-zealous traffic management. Like improvisation skills we need to be ready for anything not try to be ready for everything.

Townsend, Robert

Up the Organisation: How to Stop the Corporation from Stifling People and Strangling Profits Michael Joseph (May 1970)

So what can a book written nearly half a century ago, about Avis, teach us today? Astonishingly a lot. It's fresh, direct and simple. Way to go.

Welch, Jack

Jack: What I've Learned Leading a Great Company and Great People Headline Book Publishing (22 December 2003)

Reading Titans of industry telling us how great they were palls but this still has plenty of good stuff. More Gretzky (the ice hockey player) than Aristotle perhaps. Key lessons: get the people right, set tough targets and have rigorous systems. He says he wants his people to embrace 'speed, simplicity and self-confidence'. Action this day....

Wipperfurth, Alex

Brand Hijack: Marketing without Marketing Portfolio (3 January 2005)

He argues marketing hasn't changed enough and lives in the past. He argues brands need to lighten up and have a sense of humour. He says it's about telling the audience exactly what they want to hear but don't know until they hear it. A good book.

Wiseman, Richard

Did You Spot the Gorilla? How to Spot Hidden Opportunities Arrow Books (5 August 2004)

In general graphic *'how to be a success in 30 minutes'* guide books are a turn-off for me but Wiseman (as his name might suggest) has some interesting experiments he's conducted.

What did you think of this book?

We're really keen to hear from you about this book, so that we can make our publishing even better.

Please log on to the following website and leave us your feedback.

It will only take a few minutes and your thoughts are invaluable to us.

www.pearsoned.co.uk/bookfeedback

Index

.